SEX
IS MORE THAN A
PLUMBING LESSON

a parents' guide to sexuality education
for infants through the teen years

Patty Stark

Published by Preston Hollow Enterprises, Inc.
P.O. Box 670935
Dallas, Texas 75367-0935

Second Printing: 1992

Cover design by Michele Renault

ISBN:0-9629463-0-3

The author gratefully acknowledges permission to reprint excerpts from the following:
Adams, G., Adams-Taylor, S. & Pittman, K. (1989). Adolescent Pregnancy and Parenthood: A Review of the Problem, Solutions, and Resources. Family Relations, 38, p. 225. Copyright © (1989) by the National Council on Family Relations, 3989 Central Ave. N.E., Suite #550, Minneapolis, MN 55421. Reprinted by permission.

Acknowledgements

I have been fortunate to have had a few supportive people in my life during critical periods of my journey. Each of them has contributed to this work by loving me.

To those who were my cheerleaders and honest critics as I wrote, I thank each of you: My treasured brother, George Anton, and "lifetime" friends, Chip & Anna Fichtner, Jennifer & Randy Runyeon.

I am eternally grateful for the wonderfully spiritual and intellectual women in my life. Kathy Herring shares my vision for the rich and unlimited potential of the human soul, lives the vision, and inspires me. Karen Smith embraces the world and never forgets to laugh. Corinne Swaney sets her sights high and engages her energy and principles to reach them. Kay Frigo, challenges her senior high school "gentlemen" to look beyond immediate gratification and to understand what gives our sexuality its meaning.

Brilliant Balu Prabhakar offered me countless hours of technical assistance. No challenge overwhelmed him.

And to Ricky, my dear friend, mentor and guide, my "starmn"...

Our goal is to raise children who know their worth and who will care for themselves, including their bodies.

Contents

What distinguishes human sexual touching is our ability to take that activity beyond a mere arousal response - to communicate honest emotional caring and commitment.

Preface

No matter the age of your child when you first pick up this book, I suggest that you read it from beginning to end. Although you may think that the chapters dedicated to toddlers and small school-age children do not apply to your preteen or teen, they do. There is a continuum of knowledge and a basic philosophy underlying the entire work. You will get a more comprehensive understanding of this perspective if you start at the beginning.

These chapters are not simple questions with answers for what to say to your child when (s)he asks a specific question about sex at a certain age. For example, how the mother of a six-year-old might answer a question about family planning methods would be very different than that of a parent of a sixteen-year-old who may be sexually active. Rather, this is a collection of information and knowledge from many sources, each making contributions to our understanding of how human beings learn to have positive and responsible attitudes about their sexuality and their interactions with others.

These chapters are about empowering you as a parent to be successful at communicating a vision of human sexuality which reflects your personal values, culture, and knowledge. There is an abundance of materials out right now that delivers facts about sexual subjects, but none of these can accurately present its information within the context of your unique beliefs, wisdom, and values gained from your life experiences.

If you and your child are beginning this process while your child is young, then you are both fortunate. However, if this is a part of parenting which you have postponed, keep in mind that we are amazingly resilient beings, and that your child can truly benefit from your attention to sexuality starting right now. After all, one's sexual development is a lifelong process.

Human sexuality is rich not because of acts and gestures performed in a vacuum but because of the meaning which we attach to these actions. As a parent, you help your child establish a sense of his/her place within your family and larger communities. Now, if you have not already started, it is time to begin the lengthy and gradual process of helping your child to clarify who (s)he is as a sexual being and how to express and enjoy that miracle in healthful, life-enhancing ways.

Introduction

Over one million teenage girls become pregnant in the United States each year. That probably means that at least one million of our teenage sons father babies each year. Repeatedly we read of the high frequency of abortion and divorce, the growing incidence of sexually transmitted diseases (STDs) and teen suicides, and the unfortunate prospects for teen mothers, their children, and their extended families. Everyone believes that sex education is important and necessary, but there is little agreement about <u>how</u> to provide it, <u>when</u> and <u>where</u> to teach it, and most importantly, <u>what</u> to include.

There is only one aspect of sex education that everyone--government, educators, population control people, religious leaders, adults, <u>and</u> teenagers--agrees upon: parents should be their children's primary sex educators. Unfortunately, in most households, they are not.

There was a time when parents didn't need to be so concerned about carefully articulating their knowledge and beliefs about sexuality. There was general support for one form of sexual expression: sexual intercourse was the exclusive privilege of heterosexual married couples. Prior to television and modern film, sex and marriage were usually portrayed as Siamese twins; you didn't get one without the other. The rules were pretty clear, generally accepted, and supported. So children grew up witnessing a consistent ethic. When there was a violation of that ethic (e.g., Daddy had a mistress), it was usually kept quiet and was a source of embarrassment, even shame, to family members--proof that unsanctioned sexual relationships brought about pain and disappointment. In other words, there were definite societal values with systems in place (formal and informal) to support and enforce them.

Along with these standards for behavior, our agrarian economy kept the population intimately acquainted with the processes of life, survival, and death. Animals mating and birthing provided ready information and occasions for children's curiosity to be stimulated and addressed. Babies birthed and/or nursed at home were promptings for questions and answers. So the learning about sex was enveloped in the learning about life. "Sex education" was not a separate subject created to address an urgent social problem. It was part of the total life experience, no different than learning about weaving, planting, cooking, and securing fuel for harsh winters.

We no longer live in those times. While we humans have not changed all that much as a species, our philosophies and activities have taken vast leaps in just half a century:

- Sex, which was primarily focused on procreating, is now primarily recreational and relationship-enhancing.
- Whereas heterosexual, marital intercourse was once the rule, there no longer exists one, clear societal standard of sexual conduct.
- Sex roles (male and female) were narrowly defined, with most behaviors easily labeled as male or female. Today, men and women share roles which were previously restricted by gender boundaries.

- While society was once clear about which sexual practices were tolerable, by whom, and under which circumstances, children now get conflicting messages from multiple sources.

- Out-of-marriage pregnancy and "ruined reputations" were the unfortunate consequences of unsanctioned sexual practices. Today, the consequences are much higher: a plethora of sexually transmitted diseases, some life-threatening (A.I.D.S.) and lifetime (herpes), others persistent and precursors to other reproductive problems (cervical cancer). Yet there is less social support for postponing sexual intercourse and discouraging the number of sexual contacts.

Children now need comprehensive information and guidance about their sexuality from adults who may have received none themselves or who are confused, having been raised with multiple and conflicting messages. Even if we do not speak directly to our children about sex, they are absorbing numerous ideas about life, relationships, and personal expression from the world about them. Our kids are being educated about sexuality and relationships whenever they watch television or movies, listen to music, read books, newspapers and magazines, when they visit with their friends, and when they interact or simply observe us at home. What are some of their primary sources teaching them? Let's begin with most parents.

Parents

Some kids report getting "the talk," an awkward event when Mom or Dad (usually Mom for the daughter, Dad for the son, rarely both parents together) asks them to sit down in a quiet room, and they are told about menstruation or wet dreams and where babies come from. It is a trying encounter for both parent and child, and it is often ill-timed; the kid is either too old or too young, and the information provided is correspondingly too little or too much. The parent prays that the child does not ask any questions and if the child does, the parent replies with as vague an answer as possible.

Others report learning absolutely nothing from their parents. Unfortunately, most kids fall into this category. Sex is never or rarely discussed. There is an unspoken understanding that sex is not a topic for polite conversation, at least not in this house. Some kids ask their parents questions, really needing answers and, at best, get a humorous answer which still says: "Let's not talk about this." So nobody says anything, and young children who lack other sources imagine all sorts of ridiculous and terrifying things:

- "I know that my folks have only 'done it' three times because there are only three kids in our family."
- "I might have cancer; there's blood coming out of my bottom, and I haven't had an injury."

Gradually, both those who get the bare bones facts and those who get nothing tend to pick up their information about sex from other sources, reliable or not. No other area of life is treated so strangely for the passing along of normal life information and ideas.

This silence and isolation of sex to a one-time or occasional fact-cramming session communicate one thing very strongly: something is "different" about sex--maybe weird, maybe dangerous, maybe naughty, but it is not an okay subject. We talk about death, auto insurance, dental visits, divorce, and body odor in our daily conversations, but we set our sexuality off in a corner and indicate that it is separate and must remain so: off limits or, at best, minimally addressed.

This extreme attitude, ignoring and isolating a fundamental element of our human experience (our sexuality), creates a major problem: we communicate that our sexual nature is unacceptable. When we exclude this basic ingredient during our children's formative years, we fragment their identities, because we are refusing to look at them, and ourselves, as whole people with male and female dimensions.

The Entertainment Media

Another source for children being educated about sexuality is the entertainment industry, which provides a sharp contrast to the parental model of saying nothing or saying little. Mass communication systems, such as TV and film, typically teach kids that love is a feeling that we experience shortly after meeting an attractive man/woman. We best express this new "love" through sexual intercourse, an act we now describe as "making love," though real love may have nothing to do with it. This event, we observe, has almost no relationship to family planning and babies, requires no cleaning-up afterward, and can be repeatedly performed by handsome men each time they are in bed with beautiful women. Married people are oftentimes portrayed as bored with each other and no longer participants in the world of passion, so they are usually excluded from romantic roles and scenes. In the rare event that married couples do display some hint of happiness and attraction, they normally are able to achieve this status because there are no kids living in the house. Oh, and one more thing, when "lovers" awaken the next morning, they look fantastic and never have bad breath.

Music, too, has been a prominent sex educator. Children and adolescents learn that once aroused, they <u>must</u> have sex with their partners ("...just got to have you, Baby," or "can't wait another minute" or "I can't resist your touch"), and that they are incomplete, pathetic little nothings without a partner's love. More recently, we get the message that women are objects for sexual gratification, and there is an increase in suggestions for the use of force with women during sex. Does that mean they still call it "making love"?

Their Friends

Somewhere in the middle are our children's friends who teach each other such "facts" as the following:

- Douching with a cola can keep you from getting pregnant.
- If you stand up during sex you can't get pregnant. This method is "more dependable" if you wear high-heel shoes.
- You can't get pregnant the first time you have sexual intercourse (about a fifth of girls do, however).

• You can tell if a guy really loves you because his eyes will be dilated (they confuse arousal with love).

We can continue to rely on these constant sources of misinformation and then complain about children's confusion and the high rate of teen pregnancies, births and abortions, STDs, and emotional damage, or we can equip ourselves to do the job of educating our children ourselves. When we fail to give them the facts and share <u>our values</u> with them, we deny them an important part of their identity as emerging men and women, and we deny them important information for making responsible choices. We also deny ourselves a rich opportunity to be closer to them.

Is it neglect or abuse when a parent permits a toddler to roam the beach unattended, watching the inviting water and others safely at play? Knowing what we do about the physical and emotional hazards of early sexual experimentation, are we neglectful or abusive as a nation when we dangle hours and hours of sexually provocative lifestyles before our children without balancing the fantasy with useful training in the analysis and behaviors they will need to make sound decisions which contribute to their health and lifegoals?

There is no substitute for you, your child's parent. You are the critical person, the irreplaceable professional who must, and can, help your child understand the many and confusing messages about sexuality. No one else has the years of bonding with your child that you have. No one else knows your child as well as you do, and no one else can translate <u>your</u> values to your child the way you can in the everyday context of family life.

There is encouragement from researchers whose preliminary findings indicate that parents and children who are good communicators about sexual issues get better results: the teenagers have more accurate information about sex, are more open with their parents, have a better understanding of their parents' attitudes and values, and tend to postpone sexual involvement until they are older. Parents who serve as the major sources for their children's sexual information have children who are less sexually active, have fewer sex partners, and are more consistent and effective contraceptors when they do become "sexually active." When it comes to discussing sexual matters at home, openness fosters more responsible attitudes and behaviors and contributes to an environment where children's self-regard is strengthened.

Parents are a critical component in successful sexuality education because it involves so much more than understanding the mechanics of genital behavior, reproduction, and family planning. That is why school courses cannot successfully perform the task of sexuality education alone. Arithmetic can be taught in school without any assistance from a parent (although parental involvement expedites the process) because it involves learning a specific body of information and its application. Unlike school subjects, learning about sexuality is a lifetime process about discovering who we are and how we will express ourselves in many ways and situations, with just one of them being genital.

Picking up this book is a major step, and it is written to make the subsequent ones much easier. First, I want to assist you in getting comfortable with your role as sex educator. Actually, it is a job you have been doing ever since you began parenting, but you may not have realized it. When we teach our small children the differences between boys and girls, that's sex education. When we teach our children how to use the bathroom and keep themselves clean, how to express themselves and relate to other people, that's sex education. It is education about our sexuality, and our sexuality is who we are as males or females. You have started the job; now I want to help you proceed as the messages become more complex, more emotionally charged, more challenging for our kids and for us as parents.

We have been told repeatedly that it is up to us to teach our children about sex, but no one has ever taught us how to teach our children. With some help and a little advance preparation and thought, sexuality teaching is a manageable and even exciting part of parenting.

In this book, we will look at our own attitudes about sexuality, our personal values, how we relate to our children so that we can communicate about sex and other subjects, and we will look at developmental stages and how those relate to sexuality education. Within each chapter, you will find discussions, questions, and suggestions which might be helpful to you in understanding your own feelings and beliefs surrounding the many issues and attitudes related to human sexuality. These will facilitate the communication of your knowledge and values to your children, perhaps making it easier for you to hear their needs and beliefs (which will constantly change as they develop) and enrich each other's lives. If these are helpful, great. If not, use your own imagination and experiences, and carry on.

I admire and congratulate every parent willing to be the major source of a child's knowledge about him/herself and the complicated world of sexual communication. We have spent years insisting that "somebody ought to teach kids about sex." Thanks for deciding to be that "somebody." I feel good about making this journey with you.

Chapter One

IF SEXUALITY ISN'T JUST "SEX," WHAT IS IT?

We have become stuck in the limited ways that we think about sex. "Sexuality," "sexually active," "sexy." Just about any word whose root is "sex" is usually interpreted as being synonymous with genital stimulation and little more. We forget that there is a whole lot more to sexual matters than those thoughts, feelings, and acts associated with genital arousal and satisfaction.

Sexuality is a broad, unlimited concept, because each human being's potential is limitless. Sexuality is about who we are as girls and boys, men and women and how we express ourselves. That is why one's sexuality is very unique, very individual. I express my femaleness, my feminine sexuality, in a way that is personally my own. Those around me observe my sexuality through my choices in clothing, friends, music, vacations, and literature. My sexuality is manifested in my tones of voice, facial expressions, moods, expressed emotions, and parenting style. My husband is in touch with different aspects of my sexuality than are my parents or siblings. And some friends know more about who this woman is than others.

Rather than being an established, stagnant set of characteristics, one's sexuality is the nature of the person, an on-going, evolving process of being, becoming, and expressing. The maleness and femaleness which we communicate is influenced by our environments and limited only by the intellectual, emotional, and spiritual forces within us.

A helpful example of this concept can be found in the differences among men. Some adult males are emotionally distanced. They do not express their feelings, and they demonstrate little interest in or understanding of others' emotional experiences. These men express a different sexuality than those men who are more open in their friendships and where personal exchanges are more prevalent. Both groups are males, adults, perhaps financial contributors to families and communities, and both contain members who experience satisfying sex lives. Yet they express themselves very differently to themselves and to those around them.

It is this identity and how it is communicated that is the essence of our human sexuality. As there are as many different identities as there are people, there is no <u>one</u> male sexuality nor one female sexuality. Are there similarities within each gender as to how we disclose our sexuality? Of course. And do most of us include the use of our genitals in expressing ourselves with some person(s) at some stage(s) of our lives? Absolutely. But beyond the similarities are subtle nuances which make each of us a unique sexual being.

Is sexuality about intercourse? Yes, partly. And as you can see, it is about so much more. As we pursue the challenging task of teaching our children about their sexuality, let us keep in mind that we are communicating about who we and they are as people in the lifetime process of growth. The focus of this book is on how our sexual identities impact our choices and feelings regarding genital sexual attitudes and behaviors. It is written to urge and empower families to celebrate their creative powers and to become the generous lovers we are meant to be.

Chapter Two

OUR BODIES, THEIR BODIES

An important place to begin, when considering the spoken and unspoken ways we communicate to our children about human sexuality, is with our attitudes about our bodies. From infancy, children mimic our behaviors. Boys and girls will posture themselves in the bathroom exactly as their fathers do each morning when shaving and will imitate skin care routines which they observe their mothers performing. So when children see us liking and caring for our bodies, appreciating them as they are, they get the message that their bodies are good, too.

This is particularly challenging for us because at this time in our society, there are strong and regular reminders convincing us that we should be physically "perfect." Especially for women, the standard for "perfection" changes every few seasons (e.g., thin, boyish bodies; thin athletic bodies; thin athletic bodies with large bosoms; curvy sensuous bodies...). Men, also, are increasingly affected by these messages. Pretty is not just as "pretty does"; "pretty" is heavily determined by body shape, size, and adornments. The challenge for us is considerable. With daily directives for achieving "just the right look" and equal reminders of the many ways we fall short of physical perfection, many of us must struggle to actually _feel_ good about our bodies, accept them as they are, and then translate that contentedness to those around us--especially our children.

There are ways in which we can influence our children to love themselves as they are, including their bodies, but first we must examine our attitudes, of which we may or may not be aware.

Parents who are comfortable with their bodies and their sexuality usually communicate the same to their children, from early childhood through adolescence. Their hygiene is good. They keep themselves covered when appropriate but don't panic when someone happens to observe them undressed (they casually cover themselves and carry on), and they are accepting and uncritical of their bodies. Their children do not get the message that genitals are dirty or untouchable. Rather, these children learn that caring for one's body and being comfortable with it is healthy--no big deal, just okay.

Children are born with no attitudes about the physical body. Any ideas that they get about certain parts being disgusting or ugly are all foisted upon them by their early caretakers and later by those who influence them from outside. In fact, prior to birth, humans usually have only positive body associations. We have never known hunger, cold, excessive heat, or hurtful touching. When we are in our fetal stage of development, we seek pleasurable experiences and avoid painful ones. I am told that scientists have observed fetal boys fondling their genitals and both sexes thumb sucking. We know, until we are taught otherwise, that our bodies can give us pleasure. Hurt, shame, and revulsion are not a part of our consciousness until we are taught those responses.

I think that we are oftentimes unaware of the ways we have adopted others' negative body associations. But they show up in many ways. I met a woman I know walking with her five-year-old daughter by her side and pushing her newborn baby in a buggy. I commented to the mother about how good she looked. While responding that she was feeling fine and was delighted with her baby, she proceeded to tell me about the awful weight she now needed to lose, her "big boobs" filled with milk, and about the "disgusting" discharge she had (i.e., the uterus emptying itself following delivery), all necessary but, to her, regrettable consequences of pregnancy and childbirth. This scene is not at all unusual.

What was this woman's daughter learning about these uniquely feminine functions? That women's bodies are remarkable? Had I been a child, I believe I would have dreaded what my body had in store for me. And why was my acquaintance so repulsed by her body and its processes? Where did she pick up these negative associations?

From that encounter, my mind began imagining typical family scenes in so many of our homes where negative body images are the norm, especially when they concern our genitals. Is there alarm and sharp correction when daughters rock themselves with their fingers in their panties while engrossed in a story being read to them? Are little boys threatened with punishment or shamed when they fondle their genitals before drifting off to sleep? Are they also chastised for the comfort they receive from rubbing a cheek, scalp, or blanket, or is that okay because they haven't touched "down there"? Are they given the message that their bowel movements are normal, and that our bodies have efficient systems for disposing of our waste? Or does the communication go beyond, making the child feel that his/her body has expelled something for which (s)he should feel embarrassed? Are maturing adolescents teased about their changing bodies, intensifying already awkward feelings?

I constantly witness the burdens that girls and women experience because of their poor body images and revulsion with their reproductive and eliminative functioning. We have been taught that menstrual periods are viewed with disgust and are called "the curse"; the elimination of body waste (even underarm perspiration) is somehow unfeminine. Many adolescent girls would rather die than have anyone know that they are menstruating, and some will painfully let hours pass on a date without using the bathroom rather than reveal that they, too, urinate and defecate. One woman told me that after dating a man for a considerable period of time and managing never to use the restroom, he finally asked her with alarm: "Don't you ever have to go to the bathroom?" She told me that she was relieved by his question because it conveyed an expectation and acceptance for women's need to relieve themselves. Why should any human being be embarrassed about such a basic physical need?

She didn't emerge from the womb with a hang-up about her body's functions, and probably no one ever said to her: "Don't use the bathroom on a date because boys don't know that girls have to go." She got that notion in subtle ways and acted on it to preserve a distorted image. They can be found in any social or economic group: women who cannot use public restrooms without the water running in the sink or the toilet flushing (to mask the tinkling noise), without smoking a cigarette (to mask any odor), or without waiting for the restroom to be empty of all other people.

High school girls with whom I have worked have accepted as an unfortunate truth advertisers' convincing message: female genitals stink. The "word from our sponsor" is that our genitals are so foul that normal washing can't possibly keep odors at bay, so the smart woman (who wishes neither to offend nor be embarrassed) accepts the generous help of corporations: she purchases and uses feminine hygiene deodorants and douches--which not infrequently upset the ecological balance of her vagina and result in irritation and infections. How can a girl feel good about the most feminine parts of her anatomy if both her public and personal sources of information are telling her that, without constant commercial help, she is offensive and will be rejected?

We are all exposed to media models who complain about their bodies and then find instant relief after they start using a product which someone recommends to them in a commercial on television. Once purchased and used, these products change their lives, so they tell us. The "problems" are ones to which each of us can relate, so that we are likely to purchase the merchandise. The message is repeated over and over again: we are never quite okay; we can always use a little help to fix things--especially as we get older or heavier. The deeper, more lasting message is that we must be hyper-vigilant about our imperfections and quick to remedy them so that others will accept us, and we will be happy. As a result, we are extremely self-critical, and this is what we model to our children who are then, in turn, anxious, insecure, and doubtfilled about themselves.

This is no way to love ourselves, and it is not a healthful model for children.

With a Smile and a Song...

Boys and girls must see their parents and other healthy adult models reveal self-acceptance and self-love. Children gather most of their information by observation. They, then, repeat the observed behavior until they have mastered it. So when we demonstrate to them that being an adult means being content with and appreciative of our bodies, they internalize that message and imitate it. These children become the adults whose happiness is generated from within, not from others' opinions, potions, and products. Unless we are able to demonstrate our own satisfaction with who we are and who they are, we will never be convincing models for self-acceptance and happiness. As mothers and fathers who want our children to be happy, we must make efforts to demonstrate gratitude for who we are and for our own special styles. There are countless everyday opportunities to feel and exhibit appreciation, respect, and delight in the miracle of our bodies. We need to seize those occasions and capitalize on them or start creating them:

- When someone compliments you about your appearance, limit your response to only words that convey appreciation for the remark: "Thank you," or "That's certainly nice to hear," or "Oh, and I'm feeling wonderful too." There's no need to downplay the compliment with remarks about needing to lose weight, the age of your garment, etc. Enjoy it; you deserve it.

- Put on clothing each day that makes you feel beautiful/handsome. Clothes which make us feel attractive are not necessarily expensive. It's the style and colors that enhance our good feelings. You don't have to dress well only for "special." Everyday is special if you're committed to making it so.

- Many parents drive all over town to get their kids to soccer, ballet, piano, etc., yet never have time for their own aerobics class, daily walk, or bubble bath. Your children need time for enrichment, and so do you. Flight attendants advise parents with infants that the parents must use the oxygen mask first so that the parents are conscious to then administer oxygen to their little ones. So give your body the attention and activities it needs to stay healthy for you--and for your role as parent.

- Kids need help to understand the power of advertising messages. What is fact? How are words and images used to create self-doubts, needs, and desires? You and your children can make a game of dissecting advertisements to increase their awareness of how and when we are influenced. Kids love analyzing ads; it's a form of playing detective in the real world.

● Stand in front of the mirror each morning and make a positive statement about yourself. Smile as you say: "Gosh, I'm good looking," or "My teeth are one of my best assets." I know one woman who remarks that stretch marks are among her "merit badges" earned while she was working on her "baby badges."

● If you are having negative thoughts about your body, take four immediate steps: (1) refrain from verbalizing the negative thought (especially in front of your child); (2) focus on another part of your body which satisfies you; (3) aloud, make a positive remark about that bodypart on which you have placed your focus; and (4) reward yourself immediately (e.g., a quarter in your "positive thinking" jar).

● Seek out men and women who are content, happy, and affirming with themselves and with you. We saw a musician perform recently with the Dallas Symphony Orchestra, and I was so attracted to her. Her clothing and body movements communicated a wondrous comfort with her gender, age, work, and body. She did not <u>talk</u> about contentment; she <u>modeled</u> it.

She was such a contrast to the men and women who are obsessed with body fat and wrinkles, who will never be satisfied with their appearances--never. Do they represent emotional freedom, or are they the products of a culture which worships youth, svelte bodies, smooth skin, and trends which change just as soon as we've purchased all the right items? What image of womanhood/manhood are they giving to others and, more importantly, to the next generation?

There is a very good reason why small children love Mr. Rogers, the television personality. In a world that is moving awfully fast and where the demands for performance are tremendous, even for little kids, Mr. Rogers is a daily model of positive self-regard. He assures children that they don't need to do anything or change anything to have his love. I believe that his messages are profound models for positive parenting.

Our children deserve healthy models and teachers. They need information about how their bodies will change and how they can best care for them, but they need more than that. The information must be presented with the backing of an attitude that says: "I appreciate my healthy body and its remarkable, synchronized functions, and yours is pretty incredible, too."

We know children who are aware of their mother's body attitudes, not from any formal talks, just by observation and conversation. They know that she menstruates and that her daughters will, too, one day. They know that they were breastfed not only because mothers' milk is superior nutrition for infants, but because it was also good for their mother's body's recovery following pregnancy. These kids know that their mother loved holding them close to her, and she still does. They see her care for her body through exercise, healthful and moderate food choices, an occasional massage and manicure, and regular hygiene. She feeds her skin with moisturizer and, more importantly, hugs and cuddling. And they also know that in private moments, their father and mother share an exclusive intimacy.

Such parents could not be giving their children this positive dimension of human sexuality if they were not accepting of themselves. They could not appreciate their bodies and those of their children if they were fixated on "imperfections."

We tell our children about the world's wonders with voices that reveal awe. Let's tell them about their bodies and our bodies with that same reverence and enthusiasm. After all, once they reach puberty, our children are going to have these adult bodies for the rest of their lives. That's a long time to be repulsed or displeased by your very own self, or it can be a long time to be content and happy about the ways our bodies appear, function, and bring us pleasure.

For those adults who did not get positive messages about their bodies when they were children, getting those good attitudes is a process. Our own efforts, coupled with the love, patience, and honest affirmation of others, are valuable contributions to helping us let go of old, crippling ideas. Next, we must learn to communicate those good feelings about ourselves to ourselves. And finally, when we are more content with who we are, as we are, we become more satisfied with others as they are.

Parents want their children to experience personal satisfaction and peace, the foundation of happy living. Serenity cannot be purchased in response to a television commercial or magazine advertisement; nor can we instruct our children to secure it by delivering well-outlined, logical presentations on self-improvement. We must demonstrate the self-satisfaction which is the source of our own inner peace, and we must communicate to them that they are wonderful and lovable just the way they are.

Of course, our ability to do this daily is only possible if we believe in our own goodness and worth and that of our kids. For some, that positive self-regard has always been there; others must take active steps to find it. Once self-love is ours, it is also our children's for observation. Then we can hope that in their own time and special way they will acquire what we have: that inner knowing that it's okay to love ourselves, including our bodies... <u>everything</u> about them.

Chapter Three

CHECKING OUT YOUR RQ *

You are your child's primary role models for adulthood, and you perform this job not by your lectures but mainly by your informal, daily interactions which your child observes. A very important aspect of sexuality education for you to consider is what you may be communicating in your life about the relationship between love and romance. A major teen complaint about sexuality education is that it is usually a series of lessons about biological facts ("plumbing lessons") with little or no attention given to how all of that information is related to personal growth and romantic relationships.

Our immediate response as a society is to ask ourselves: "Well, what should we <u>tell</u> our children about the connection between sex and romance?" We're overlooking our most powerful instructional materials: ourselves!

What are your children learning about romance as they watch you? From very early, children observe us and gather lots of information about what it means to be "romantic," even though they don't take copious notes or <u>consciously</u> think: "Gee, that was a cool move on Mom's part last night, pretty romantic!" Then, at some point, no matter what we might prefer, nature tells kids it is time to have their own mating urges. So like the young of all species, human offspring pattern many of their mating rituals after the ones they have observed in their elders.

*   **Romance Quotient**

Romance in our private, day-to-day lives is as varied as in novels, television, and movies. Each of those media creates ideas about romance and then portrays the themes for commercial distribution (to make money). The idea which you are creating in your private relationships is, presumably, for your personal enjoyment and the enhancement of your relationship. However, if you have children, your romantic concept is being "distributed" to those in your immediate circle: mainly, the children in your life.

How do you keep romance alive in your relationship(s), and what are children absorbing about attraction, friendship, love, and commitment in romantic involvements?

Some parents decide that it is best not to touch each other in front of the children. They figure that if the children see how much happiness and pleasure their love relationship brings them, then the kids will be in too big of a hurry to go out and get their own pleasure. You have heard it before: "They'll just get ideas." For others, the decision to refrain from affection in front of the children is a convenient excuse to avoid looking at the dynamics of the marriage relationship. With some couples, it is a symptom of underlying hostilities and unresolved issues; and until those concerns are addressed, they serve as a wedge which precludes the enjoyment of tender gestures.

For many, marital affection is absent because the partners have never learned how to be casual, playful, affectionate lovers. So the kids become the excuse. These couples have never gotten into a pattern of expressing affection except when sexual intercourse is on the agenda. In fact, I have had women tell me (and surely there are men in similar situations) that, for their husbands, if any sort of touching takes place (a kiss, a prolonged hug at the door, a pat on the rear), intercourse <u>must</u> follow. In those marriages, the women avoid tenderness with their husbands because touching always has a limited purpose: a preface to intercourse. Frustrated by this utilitarian approach, they long for the playfulness of years before or of other relationships.

Of course there are lots of other reasons that parents fail to demonstrate affection in front of their children, but the point is that there are many households where children never or rarely witness tender (but <u>appropriate</u>) physical contact and words between the parents. The concept that they absorb is that married people's lives lack spark, spontaneity, and fun; life just goes on day after day.

For these kids books, music, movies, and television offer another view of romance in relationships which is much more inviting. The commercial media have a profit motive, and over the years they have learned that if they fill the scenes with passionate and explicit scenes, the profits increase dramatically.

A major problem with our children's constant exposure to that single approach is that these media have not successfully portrayed much beyond infatuation or desire, then arousal and, finally, orgasm. There is not enough time to portray the gradual development and nurturing of love relationships in movies or television programs with commercial interruptions, so sexual acts are substituted. A result is that the viewer confuses two very individual life events: choosing to love and choosing to engage in genital acts of pleasuring. So, for young audiences who have little experience with the work (and the pleasures) of creating lasting love and intimacy, the primary model for romance is an activity that is all too frequently hazardous to their physical and emotional health: sexual intercourse. This model may not reflect reality, but it <u>sure</u> looks good. Our kids adopt a faulty reality that tells them that people on the screen (unlike parents) <u>understand</u> what it means to be deeply in love and to be fiercely attracted to each other, that the characters are superior models for living life happily ever after.

So what does the thinking teenager deduce from all of this? To which model is (s)he attracted? Of course, the media model. It's the appealing one. It's the one that holds out promise of good feelings, being emotionally and physically connected with another individual, looking beautiful, and feeling alive. The media models seem to have it all.

So what is the competition (you and I, Parents) offering? If we have another vision for our kids' romantic relationships, one that does not suggest sexual intercourse as a healthful option at this time in their lives, what do we do? What kind of "program of attraction" is on our life's menu?

Dorothy, in <u>The Wizard of Oz</u>, had solutions at hand (or shall I say "at foot"?) as she traveled the Yellow Brick Road in her ruby slippers, but she didn't know the magic her shoes possessed. You, too, have an abundance of knowledge and experience, perhaps from many years ago, that can now add zip to your love life and which can model a broad range of imaginative styles for building and sustaining romance. Maybe the time has come to relocate these talents and pull them out of the mothballs.

A Walk Down Memory Lane

Do you remember the feeling of being newly attracted to someone and having him/her express interest in you as well? That feeling is one of life's most incredible experiences. It's physical and emotional. It's total body and "out of body." There is no way to describe the sensation, the thrill, but anyone who has had it can remember. Even thinking about it is somehow electrifying. Do you recall the frequent embraces, tender exchanges of loving thoughts, the cards you sent each other, the unexpected, "no-special-reason-other-than-I-love-you" gifts you presented? Is there a place in your memory that harbors scenes of silly moments when you put your cares aside and focused only on each other? Most of us had job, school, and/or family responsibilities back then but nothing, absolutely <u>nothing</u>, got in the way of our romance.

Are you still getting those charges from your relationship? If not, what happened to them?

Those special behaviors, usually unique to new romances, do not end abruptly. There is a very gradual process during which we attend to more "urgent" or "important" needs at the expense of our now-familiar relationship and its needs and wants. And ever so slowly, we get out of the habit of being new lovers. By the time our children are old enough to notice we, all too frequently, have lost the magic touch and have only vague memories of how neat life was "back when."

Well, just as we got out of the habit of making small, daily choices to set aside the time to enjoy the sweet nothings which added spark and zest to our love lives, we can now make new daily choices to reinstitute them. Now please, do not begin by making big plans to kidnap your beloved at work and whisk him/her off to a fancy hotel room with a big bathtub; there is no way you can maintain that pace. That feeling which you hope to recapture can best be recreated and maintained by elements which already exist in your day-to-day environment. If you are dependent upon super-events (e.g., long week-ends in San Francisco, candlelight dinners at your area's most expensive restaurant, losing forty-five pounds, purchasing the perfect wardrobe), it will not work, because super-events cannot be woven into the texture of your daily lives.

Instead, go back to those memories. What do you recall as your light, love-enriching moments? What sorts of things did you do for or with him/her that made both of you feel loved. I am not talking about the things which made you both feel aroused; I'm referring to the tender moments, words, expressions, and small gestures which made you feel close to each other. Did you snuggle on the couch and just dream together? Did you take long walks holding hands? Did you window shop? Wrestle and giggle? Go to playgrounds? Prepare special dinners and eat by candlelight? Call one another in the middle of the day just to say, "I love you"? Did you buy suggestive greeting cards and mail them to his/her house or office?

You may respond, "(S)he doesn't care about that anymore," or "Ah, there's just not time for those things anymore; besides real parents don't do stuff like that." Want to bet? If a local radio station announced that free vacations to Hawaii were being given to couples who spent thirty minutes each day for a month romancing each other, do you think you would find the time? Just because your parents may not have romanced each other does not mean that their way is the <u>only</u> way to live as a loving couple. It can be done; but to succeed you must <u>want</u> to have that special time back in your lives and make it a priority.

Although they may not articulate them clearly to us, children pick up on much of the non-verbal communication in our homes. When romance between their parents is not visible at home but is constantly visible between unmarrieds around them and on the screen, young children and teens quickly conclude that the fun is over once you are married. That being the case, they had better experience the good times while they can and emulate the actors and actresses.

What kind of advertisement is that for committed love? What we are telling our children is that marriage kills romance. Marriage doesn't kill those romances; the couple's daily choices slowly extinguish the light of their love.

Everybody Wins

When romance is alive and well in their parents' marriages, children see that the playfulness and tenderness that always look so thrilling in the movies can continue throughout the married years, and that the romance even gets better. Kids who observe loving activities between their parents learn that the language of love is more than the passionate sexual intercourse without commitment that has been their primary and frequent model because of the mass media. Instead, they see that married love is teeming with exciting possibilities.

Do you recall the acronym, "P.D.A."? It stands for public display of affection--the kind of stuff that young lovers do because it's just so great being together, kissing a lot, hugging no matter where we are. That is the sort of touching that I am talking about being comfortable doing in front of our children. French kissing and intimate fondling are private forms of sexual communication, not meant for others to view. But as bright human beings, we are capable of redeveloping an appropriate romantic repertoire which can enliven our feelings for our beloved and provide a marvelous model for our kids.

There is an important principle which child development and family health specialists like to have people remember: When conscientious parents make their marriage their first priority, their children feel especially secure. So, when children see that romance is alive and well in their parents' marriage, they can point to specific behaviors which testify to a healthy relationship, playfulness and joy, contributing to harmony in the household for all. This translates to: "Mom and Dad must love each other, so they are going to stay married." That is awfully reassuring to children, whether they are small or teens ready to take off for college or careers.

To make time for romance is a choice which says that you value the relationship, and that you are entitled to expressing your love and to receiving love throughout the day. Romance strengthens a marriage and enriches the pleasures of our intimate sexual sharing. When our children observe our love in action, they feel secure about their family situations, and we have demonstrated a variety of ways which couples have for communicating the special feelings real lovers share. We have subtly conveyed to them that the vocabulary of love is much greater than the single act of passionate intercourse.

Talking about love and reading about it are not enough to make romance come to life. The magic of intimate loving is born of a choice to be active friends and lovers, to create an exclusive connection whose magic lingers in our thoughts and feelings, whose power urges us to greatness.

So what are you waiting for? Isn't it time to turn off the tube and turn the light on again in your love life? You have created and experienced those indescribable feelings before, maybe "way back when." You know that you can redevelop the skills which once served as vehicles for creating your special world of new love. Though they may be rusty, little by little, you can renew the daily habit and establish an attractive model of what it means to be lovers...twenty-four hours a day.

Consider your child's questions as you would a friend's knock at the door – they are meant to be answered.

STARTING WITH THE LITTLE ONES

During the years while your children are small, their questions about sexual matters will be pretty simple. Getting acquainted with their big world, they seek lots of specific information about themselves and those around them (e.g., names of body parts, the place where babies grow inside of their mothers, what people do at their work).

Our focus during these years is not only to give them honest answers to their questions but also to respond to those questions in ways that help them to feel good about themselves and their bodies. Lots of children are taught to feel embarrassed or ashamed about so many aspects of childhood which are perfectly normal (e.g., not wanting to give up their bottles, not yet being toilet-trained, not wanting to share). Our goal is to raise children who know their worth and who will care well for themselves and others.

We will look at many of the areas where we have opportunities to enhance their self-regard and functioning. You are the most vital link in your child's unfolding, and how you respond as (s)he develops and explores her world will have a lasting impact on her degree of pleasure and fulfillment throughout her lifetime.

I refuse to believe that our bodies were brilliantly created but with one main flaw—our genitals.

Chapter Four

INFANTS AND TODDLERS

If you are starting this book with this chapter, you may be confused, thinking that infants and toddlers don't have anything to do with sexuality. If <u>sexuality</u> is synonymous with <u>sexual intercourse</u> for you, then that is true. However, as I have stated before, our sexuality is not merely about what we do with our genitals. Sexuality is about our maleness and our femaleness and how we experience and express those aspects of ourselves. That being the case, sexual intercourse is simply <u>one way</u> of expressing our sexuality, just as financial support is only a part of parenting.

Because our sexuality manifests itself every minute of every day (the way we dress, speak, move our bodies, etc.), we are communicating something about our image of human sexuality in each interaction with everyone, including our very small children. As our little ones have yet to exhibit interest in those aspects of sexuality which concern the mechanics of reproduction and the nuances of expressing love with a partner, what we teach them is more about their intrinsic goodness and wonder, being valued, and being members of the human family. Those ingredients become part of their inner-knowing, which they incorporate into their own sense of self and how they express the growing individuals they are. This is the foundation for the healthy child who will someday become the healthy adult, capable of a deep, lasting, and satisfying intimacy with another.

Hugs and Cuddles

Your child's earliest "sexuality education" begins with the physical care you give him/her. This is so much more than filling your child's belly, keeping her body warm, or insuring that his bottom is dry. Having emerged from a nearly perfect world (the womb) where there was neither hunger nor wet bottoms, where the temperature was perfect, and where no one fussed with clothing, your child wants and needs lots of cuddling, hugging, caressing, and rocking.

This is why child development professionals remind young parents to hold their children close to them during feeding time. We are encouraged to sing to our little ones and engage in lots of pastimes which require active participation with them. This is so much more than our merely sharing a physical space. Children whose caretakers give them abundant and consistent physical and emotional nurturing are generally healthier and more responsive.

How can this early physical nurturing possibly be related to quality sexuality education? It teaches your child from the start that he is important, that his world is a secure one, because the people in it value him and help him to meet his needs, and that it is okay for him to express his wants and needs (e.g., hunger, cold) without fear of being punished. Children, even little newborns, learn how to interact in their world and how to be in relationships by the ways in which they are reinforced or punished.

Let's take this a step further in terms of sexual behavior. The teenager who has been raised in an environment where she has been affirmed as a worthwhile person for years is more likely to feel confident and too valuable to place at risk when the pressure is on to choose behaviors which may not be appropriate for her (e.g., teen sex, drugs, skipping school, shoplifting). Much of her good self-feeling originates with the messages she received when she was cuddled and hugged. Those moments said to her: "You are such a neat human being that I want to be with you and be close to you." Those messages contained a constant theme of her great worth, which she can now translate to "worthy of great care."

Helping a child to develop high self-regard is similar to managing a bank account. If there is little or nothing in the account when you need to draw on it in moments of financial need, you are out of luck. But if you have methodically built your account during easy as well as demanding times, with your history of fiscal discipline and decision-making you have something to draw upon.

We parents help our kids build their emotional bank accounts from infancy. We hug them, seek opportunities to include them in meaningful aspects of our lives, and we give them real opportunities to become competent managers of their own lives. As they get older, our children are exposed to other individuals who will make deposits, enhancing their sense of personal worth. There will be those, too, who will give children a taste of withdrawals: unkind remarks or exclusions (e.g., "We don't want you to play with us").

Finally, children can become their own depositors when permitted to assume increasing degrees of personal responsibility. They will experience successes which will serve as their own hard-earned deposits for their emotional bank accounts. Their personal messages are more likely to be, "I am capable of taking good care of myself and making good decisions. I know this because I already have practice doing so," or "My decision to do _____ didn't work out so well, but I sure am glad that I figured how to resolve that situation."

Any boy or girl, who along with family and friends, has been building such a fund from deposits of love, caring, acceptance, and personal responsibility, will be much better situated when some of the rough times come along, especially during the teen years. Because such children have a deep understanding of how very special they are, they have a better chance of making decisions that reflect a higher sense of personal worth; they do not squander their health, circumstances, and futures so readily as kids who think that they have little to lose. This all begins with the loving touches we give them in infancy.

The Magic of Touch

You know how wonderful it feels to be held, hugged, and rocked. Touching and being touched are such emotionally and physically satisfying experiences for us. After all, our skin is the body's largest organ. When we are touched in ways that make us happy and meet our needs, we feel accepted and treasured by another. Nurturing touches are vital experiences in the development of our self-acceptance, for, through others, we learn that we are valued.

What happens in our sexual development when comfortable, appropriate, nurturing touching is scant or absent? We may easily become emotionally underprivileged, just as a child who grows up without adequate nutrition becomes malnourished. So being, we may become disruptive in order to get attention, any kind of attention, to fill that need that has not been met. Or we may learn to cope by turning inward and becoming stoical, believing that we are unaffected by the absence of physical affirmation and pleasure in our lives. But we know for a fact that the void left by this unfulfilled need will present itself in other, unexpected ways, poisoning our feelings about ourselves and our relationships with others.

I have heard people say: "Well, my dad wasn't a toucher, and I'm just not a toucher either. My kid will survive; I did." Sure they survived, but their batteries are never fully charged, and they are not among the people who are fully alive. They are rarely the ones who are warm and approachable, the kind of people we want to include in our lives, because they do not know <u>how</u> to be warm and approachable. They learned from their early experiences that life is tough, and you have to take care of yourself because you cannot count on other people to be there for you with support and affirmations. In turn, they generally are not equipped to be the supporters and intimate friends we need. Or they may desperately search for acceptance, paying any price to secure acknowledgement and love.

Cards, books, songs, movies, poems, and art all attempt to express it: life at its best is about love and emotionally connecting with other human beings. We know that children who are emotionally <u>and</u> physically nurtured become healthier and more successful adults. So go ahead. If you have not done it before, give yourself permission to take the time to sit with your child and just be close. There is no gift you can give that will so enrich another's life as to know <u>from personal experiences</u> that (s)he is precious to another, significant human being. It doesn't matter if your house is a mess. Put all of the "shoulds" in your life aside for special moments throughout each day and physically communicate to your child that (s)he is your treasure. By starting <u>now</u> you get into the habit of cuddling. When we put if off until we "have the time," we never really develop the pattern of enjoying each other from moment to moment. Until affection becomes an integral part of our daily habits, it will continue to compete with other demands and will always come out on the short end, second to shopping, cleaning, television, work, etc. Touching is a need, not an extra. Children need physical nurturing as a constant experience, not as occasional bursts of enthusiasm and interest in them.

Days filled with time for playful and mutually-enjoyable interactions will give both of you years of memories which a perfect house, the most up-to-date wardrobe on the most awesome body, a video movie, or novel can never approximate. Then remind yourself that not only does this bring you both pleasure, it is also like building an insurance policy or making deposits in that emotional bank account for the more challenging years your child has ahead of him/her. Nothing can be substituted for your loving presence and active participation.

For when your son/daughter is a teen, the toys and possessions of childhood will not be in a handy backpack to help him/her feel worthwhile and confident. Your years of love, hugs, presence, and participation will be there, with a much better chance of manifesting themselves in a self-confident, self-affirming young man or woman who knows that (s)he is too important and worthwhile to place at risk.

Self-Pleasuring

Did you know that as babies, while still in our mothers' wombs, we suck our thumbs, stroke our genitals, and generally seek comfort? Experiments with the unborn have shown that we prefer sweet liquids introduced in the amniotic fluid to sour liquids, and we will move away from sharp instruments. When humans move from the uterus to our new environment after birth, our physical sensations are largely the same, and we continue comforting and pleasuring ourselves.

For example, we need and want to suck, not only to obtain fuel for our bodies but also to calm and comfort ourselves. Sucking is a normal, pleasurable, and even necessary activity which need not be discouraged. Yet thousands of people become worried or disturbed about small children who use pacifiers, nurse frequently, or who are not yet ready to give up the bottle or breast.

We need to recognize that many of the childcare practices of the early decades of this century reflect a faulty understanding of infants and toddlers and their needs, and that we continue to be affected by those ideas. Practices such as strict nursing schedules may have seemed very rational, but human needs and feelings aren't always rational. Do you realize that most babies in the world are nursed when they indicate that they want to nurse, not according to a clock? And they do not have to explain whether they are nursing for food or for pleasure and comfort; it is simply okay to hold them close, cuddle them, and carry on. Isn't that easier for everyone?

So if your little one likes to suck a lot, then go ahead; give him something safe (e.g., mother's breast or a pacifier), and let him have at it. You both will be happier...and emotionally healthier, too. Ditto when your baby or toddler fondles his/her genitals. This is not only a part of liking one's body; fondling is also part of a child's body discovery. We all know how cute babies are when they grab or suck on their toes. Children will grab anything within their reach. So there is nothing surprising about little ones touching their genitals. It feels good.

When babies are around a year old, they are oftentimes observed pulling at and putting their hands into their diapers. When parents frown upon a child's touching of his/her genitals, the parent gives the child an early message with lasting impact: your genitals are not okay like the rest of your body. And so begins what can be a lifetime of preoccupation and shame.

I refuse to believe that these bodies of ours were created mostly okay and neat but with one major error in the equipment: our genitals. I think that such attitudes are distorted, result in damaged feelings about ourselves, and all-too-often aberrant behavior. It is now time to give them up. So when you observe your infant or toddler son's erection, don't be disturbed. It's okay. This is his natural reaction to some physical stimulation, no different than laughing when he is tickled or getting goose bumps when he is cold. And when you find your young child fondling his/her genitals around other children or adults, give a gentle reminder that there are certain activities that we do in private (using the bathroom, flossing our teeth, clipping our fingernails). Then distract your child and move along, just as you would with any of his other undertakings.

The trick here is to never make our children feel bad or ashamed about their bodies and the sensations which their bodies provide. At the same time, we like for our kids to get the message that various endeavors are appropriate in some settings while not in others (e.g., passing gas in front of others). Whether we are able to communicate this successfully depends upon our attitudes and the emotional response we exhibit when these things happen. If you can remember that what your child is doing is normal (no matter what you think your parents or neighbors may <u>think</u>), you will soon discover that you react accordingly: it's no big deal.

"What about my bobo?"

Many of us have a tendency to segregate anything we view as sexual, treating such matters differently than other aspects of our lives. This is readily evident when discussing body parts. Body parts are usually among the first words that we teach our children, and we are delighted when they use the right words for the specific parts of their bodies. But when we get to their genitals, we react just like our parents did, and we use cutesy words, or we don't label those body parts at all. We say things like "bobo" or "weanie" for a son's penis. Girls really get short-changed on this one. Not only do we decline to use words like labia, vulva, and vagina, we normally don't even substitute cutesy words for the real thing. We just call everything "down there" a "bottom," making no distinction between any of the parts.

Does this really matter? You better believe it does. When all of the body parts except for our sexual and eliminative ones get acknowledged and called by their real names, we again communicate that there is something a bit weird about sexual and elimination matters. So weird, in fact, that parents are too embarrassed to talk about it, so we talk <u>around</u> it. This is another way of saying that everything else is normal and good, except that which concerns the lower torso. Again, we are segregating these aspects of being a human being from the rest of who and what we are.

If you are having trouble being direct and saying: "This is your penis," or "This is your vulva," it is probably that you are carrying around someone else's hang-ups about the sexual parts of your body. I believe that you will find that the more you permit yourself to use the correct words, the more comfortable you will become. Your children will not think you perverted any more than they do when you call a nose a "nose."

If you were raised in an atmosphere where people were comfortable with themselves and their bodies, then you are indeed fortunate. If not, make active choices which permit your children to be freed of unnecessary hang-ups about their bodies, feelings, and experiences. In learning from you that they are good and worthy, they will be better able to value and care for themselves through the years. They will know that their bodies are good and deserving of good care.

The infant and toddler stages are not so much for teaching children about sexuality with a checklist to be covered as they are a time for parents and children to bond with each other, to establish some of the rituals of healthy relationships. These are the weeks and months of children's first social experiences, and they will develop deeply-ingrained impressions about trust and caring, impressions which will affect every relationship for the rest of their lives. The ways in which we caretakers actually express our love will profoundly impact the self-identity, the sexuality, of our children and how they express that in ways that will enrich their lives or bring them pain.

Does sexuality education really begin when our children are tiny? Without a doubt. And no matter what you are doing or not doing, whether or not you are cognizant of the messages you are communicating, you have already begun the process.

Chapter Five

PRESCHOOLERS

A young father sat reading in a chair while he waited for his preschool son, who was getting ready to shower with him. All of a sudden, a naked form leaped upon the chair, cuddled next to the dad and asked: "Daddy, sometimes does your ding-dong get all stretched out?"

Preschoolers are such exciting people, bursting with energy and wonder, and giving us a fresh, unmuddled glimpse of our world. Their inquisitive nature, unburdened by unnecessary limitations, can offer refreshing opportunities to entertain the wonders of human sexuality. The little boy, mentioned above, is a delightful example of a curious human being fascinated with his animated body and being raised in a safe and nurturing environment.

Preschoolers' interests broaden beyond the smaller, more immediate world of the toddler. They continue much of the work performed at the earlier stage while expanding their awareness, interests, and abilities. In terms of their growth, most of the suggestions from the infant and toddler stage still apply; it's as if we are adding another layer to a cake rather than putting the first one aside and starting a second.

It remains important, for example, to continue using correct vocabulary for your and your child's body parts. And your child should now be gradually taking on more aspects of self-care: dressing himself with less assistance, learning to bathe himself from head to toe, brushing her teeth a little better, tidying his room (they still need plenty of help with this one; it is an overwhelming task for a preschooler alone), placing dirty clothes in the clothes hamper, etc.

By now, your child should be toilet-trained, and that is a great convenience (only a parent knows <u>how</u> great). Remember that disruptions in your little one's life can cause him/her to regress in this area and have some "accidents." This is especially common when a new sibling is soon to be born or just born. Your child is not trying to "get back at you" for anything, nor is he being "naughty"; soiling and wetting their underwear are normal ways that small children cope with disruption.

Little kids do not have the mental ability to talk about their feelings and work through issues the way we do. Instead, their upsets surface in other behavioral ways, like bedwetting, soiling their pants, nailbiting, rocking, and whining. So if your "perfectly toilet-trained" preschooler starts having accidents, let that be a red flag that something is upsetting him. This is a time when he needs <u>reassuring</u> rather than punishing.

I know one young mother who so wishes that she had known this simple principle of children's development and behavior when her son was small and they were traveling. Because she didn't, she became annoyed when he soiled his pants, and she punished him. Of course, punishment did not help at all, but she didn't know what else to do. How much easier and better it would have been for both of them if she had known that he needed more of her attention and cuddles.

Although preschoolers seem like "little adults," they really are in transition--part baby, part child. Each developmental stage has its own tasks for the child within it to complete. Children need the space, time, and environments where they can be happily about their important work. When we allow them the time they need without rushing them, they learn to be content where they are and how they are. This is when they learn the joy of living in the moment and experiencing life as a journey with many surprising turns.

As preschoolers, children are eager to continue the exploration which surged during their toddler days. Encourage that; curious children are bright children. So the more opportunities they have to encounter their world with praise and respect for trying, the better. I urge families to view their homes as laboratories. Childproof the home environment so that there are fewer barriers to discovery for your child and fewer headaches and worries for you.

"Where do babies come from?"

Preschoolers' curiosity, which was once pretty much limited to their own bodies, will now be keenly centered on just about everybody's bodies. They will want to know where babies come out of their mothers, how boys' bodies are different from girls', why that lady has "such a big tummy and wears big dresses," why the dog has "that big red thing coming out of his penis," and why "Mommy has hair down there, but I don't." Go ahead, you can tell them, and use words that they understand. You can use books, too, to help them grasp concepts like "what Mommy's body looks like inside."

Children ask questions because they want answers. When we pretend not to hear, tell a lie ("the stork brought her to their doorstep"), or change the subject, we <u>are</u> communicating to them. We are telling them that matters relating to reproduction are somehow tainted. Consider your child's questions as you would a friend's knock at the door: they are meant to be answered.

Preschoolers usually do not ask for lots of specifics. They are very literal and do not yet have a use for too many details. So, briefly answer their inquiries, and let them lead the way. Some parents worry about telling their kids "too much." If a four-year-old asks how a car works, I can tell by the responses when she is tired of hearing details; sex is no different. Young children move to another subject or disappear when they have heard enough.

At this age, children do not require elaborate responses. Direct, concise answers do very nicely. For example:

Child: "Why does Mommy have hair down there and I don't?"

Parent: "About the time when boys and girls are getting ready to be teenagers, their bodies start changing, becoming more like adult bodies. A boy will get hair around his penis, and a girl will get hair on her labia and above, in the front. That's part of becoming a man or a woman, and someday you'll have hair there too."

With a child for whom the above is even too much, a parent might simply answer: "That's just a difference between adults and children; adults have hair down around their genitals, and little kids don't."

At this age, parents should expect that their child will ask where babies come from or specifically: "Where did I come from?" Depending on the child, answers might be variations on the following:

Parent: "When Daddy and I were feeling very close and loving, Daddy's seed and Mommy's egg came together and made a new baby, you. Because you were so tiny, you couldn't be born right away. Your body had to develop, and grow, and get stronger. So you lived inside of my uterus for about nine months, until the day you were born. All human beings start out that way."

Some kids will ask where Daddy keeps his seeds, and where Mommy's eggs are. They have asked the question, so it is time to answer. Tell them about Daddy's testicles inside of his scrotum. If they have seen Daddy without his clothes on, this will be easier to imagine, especially for little girls. This is a good time to tell little guys that their testicles do not yet make seeds, but that they will someday. Tell them about Mommy's eggs, and that little girls are born with all of their eggs (another good reason to take good care of our bodies no matter how old we are). Just as we cannot see our kidneys and lungs, we cannot see our ovaries and eggs.

Now some of them may want to know how Daddy's seeds get to Mommy's eggs. With each step, the child is leading the way, letting you know that (s)he is curious and eager for more information. This is one of the opportunities for you to subtly include your values. While some people will refer to "mates," or "the man and the woman," others will talk about making a baby in the context of marriage and refer to the "husband and wife." Now is not the time to get into a moral discourse; you will lose your child's interest if you do. However, the words you choose will influence how your child pictures the relationship in which sexual intercourse takes place and babies are made. This is just a fine example of why <u>you</u>, from a very early time, play such an important role in your child's socialization about sexuality.

Another parent might answer with more information:

Parent: "Sometimes when Daddy and I are in bed and hugging each other and feeling extra loving, we want to be very close to each other in a way that is special for married people. We touch each other in ways that make us feel very good, and Daddy puts his penis inside of my vagina. After a while, his seeds travel from his testicles, through his penis, to inside of my body. If one of my eggs has popped outside of my ovary, then maybe one of the seeds (called sperm) will meet that egg (called ovum), and a new baby will be made. Most of the time there isn't an egg there, so we don't make a new baby. But there was an egg waiting for that sperm one time, and that's when you were made."

The Conception Story

The conception story is an important part of your child's life story, and that is why she asks and <u>needs</u> to hear it. Children feel good, loved, safe, and special knowing that they began with those most important to them, and that the event was embosomed in love.

If you and the child's other parent are no longer together, it is still okay for them to hear this story in the context of love. While the relationship may now be a painful memory for you, the result of that act, this child, can be the exciting focus of the story. The same is true for children whose biological parents cannot raise them. That the biological parents' circumstances did not work out for either or both to parent this child does not diminish the wonder of that particular child's creation. Children place tremendous importance on knowing that their personal histories are special; this contributes to their knowing that they are special, too. How you address (at another time unless they ask during the same conversation) your separation from the child's other parent or the biological parents' decision to relinquish your child for adoption are separate issues. For now, this child only wants to know how babies are made-- how (s)he was made.

Sometimes children, upon hearing your answer about their beginning, may ask more about the baby growing in the uterus. They may ask if intercourse hurts or if they (the children) could become pregnant. As part of their most elementary sexuality education, children need a clear understanding that sexual intimacy is something adults do with other adults (not with children), that sex is meant to be a loving and mutually satisfying act, and that it is good and very special.

Children may ask for the same information several times, just as they request certain stories repeatedly. That they might ask more than once does not mean that you have given a sorry answer or that your child is a poor listener or slow learner. Understanding this information about their origins is very important to them and may take some time and repetition for little ones to absorb.

Likewise, they may not ask the next seemingly logical question immediately upon hearing one of your answers. Days or weeks may pass before they return with more questions. Not to worry. When they first start asking, children do not feel an urgent need for answers, anymore than they do when they ask about the whereabouts of the area wildlife during the cold winters. Sex and sexuality are part of the whole life picture which children are trying to put together. So start giving them the pieces and communicating that there are no pieces which are "different" or about which you are ashamed or embarrassed. This is about life. Just give honest answers to the best of your ability.

Get help as needed. Picture books are very useful to children who are really inquisitive to know just how this process works. I am a big fan of public libraries. They are filled with helpful people and more information designed for each age than you could possibly use. Just do your best, keeping in mind that every parent goes through this. Ask your friends what they did when their kids started asking. Your combined ideas can create some exciting ways to address these questions.

When you stop to think about it, you know a great deal. Your inexperience may lie in the area of articulating information and your beliefs. Your hesitation may be due to our socialization which oftentimes leaves us believing that we cannot possibly do an adequate job of teaching our kids about sexuality. That's untrue. Many parents who have dreaded talking about sex and relationships with their kids have made sexuality education a priority. As the Nike brand athletic shoe advertisements say, they decided to "just do it."

The important thing to remember when your child asks a question and you don't know the answer and haven't a resource nearby is to stay cool and tell them that you don't know. There will be many subjects, about which our children will inquire, where we will find ourselves saying: "Gee, I really don't know the answer to that, but I'd sure like to know, too. Let's find the answer together." When we ignore their questions or hush them, children get the idea that something is wrong, and they may be afraid to ask again.

And when your child isn't asking...

Haven't started asking? Aw, come on! Okay, maybe not. If not, then it is up to you to get them started. Kids usually are not the ones to first ask what the cow says; we tell them and then have them make animal noises before friends and family as we beam with pride. So if we can initiate questions about animal noises, why not about sexual matters?

Just as you might take your child to a construction site and say: "Janet, see that derrick on top of the building the workers are constructing?", you can also take your child to the supermarket and say: "Janet, see the lady with the big belly in the red dress at the produce display?" Then talk about the derrick or the pregnant lady and what they mean in our world.

Opportunities are all around you:

- When bathing your child. Talk about body parts and how they work. "This is your urethra. It's kind of hard for you to see, but that's where your urine comes out of your body. I always feel so much better when I urinate, don't you? That's one of the ways our bodies clean themselves..."

- When you see a pregnant lady. "Did you know that's how I looked when you were growing inside of my uterus? Pretty soon, her baby is going to be born. I hope she enjoys her baby as much as Daddy and I are enjoying you in our lives."

- When pets have litters. This is one of the neatest events you and your children can observe. Because ours is no longer an agrarian economy, few of us get a chance to watch animals being born. If a neighbor or friend's animal is having a litter, maybe they'll agree to call you. It's peaceful and synchronized, and it's sure to bring forth lots of questions in a very comfortable setting.

- While watching a television program. "Do you know why they are rushing that lady to the hospital?..."

If you look around, you will find that there are lots of opportunities for us to talk about our bodies and their functions in easy and comfortable ways with small children. Remember, they are mighty curious, unless we condition them not to be. So this can be on-going fun as your child begins wondering about a great big, wonderful part of his world.

"I'll show you mine if you'll show me yours."

That marvelous curiosity we encourage may extend to your child's friends' bodies as well. This does not mean that your child and his friends are perverts; they are normal. It helps us to remember that children engage in many activities of which we disapprove (e.g., writing on walls, infants playing with their feces). Usually, we stay pretty calm and get busy making our feelings known and instructions clear. But because "playing doctor" involves their genitals, we tend to get in a panic and become nearly hysterical, fearing that another parent might find out and forbid our children to play together, or that our kids will grow up to be deviants.

Really, this is absolutely normal behavior. Kids are curious. And their curiosity does not have a blackout between their waists and the tops of their legs. Just calmly remind them that our bodies have private places, and that we keep our clothes on when we are playing with our friends You might mention that, "Daddy and I don't take our clothes off when our friends come over." Tell them that you know that they are curious about bodies and how they work. Remember? That's <u>empathy</u>: letting them know that you <u>understand</u> their curiosity. Many suggest distracting them. Better yet, move them along to a discussion or a picture book about bodies, one that is written for small children. This affirms them for wanting to explore their world while demonstrating (rather than lecturing) a good way of going about it.

A similar occurrence is when you see (and you will) your child "playing" with him/herself around others (while watching the TV, while listening to story hour at the library, anytime). Kids fondle their genitals without even realizing it, usually because the fondling feels good. For others, fondling is a bit like thumbsucking; they find it a comfort when they are anxious. Whatever the reason, gently remind your child that touching ourselves in "places that are covered by our underwear" is okay when we do it in private, but that we don't do it in public--just like using the bathroom. No scolding, no threatening, no tension, just a gentle reminder, and maybe a distraction. A helpful comparison is nosepicking. How many times do we remind small children to use a tissue rather than their fingers? Touching their genitals in public is much the same.

Exploitation: Victims don't deserve blame.

Most of the touching and exploring children do is typical of preschool behavior, and our job is to direct them to channel it appropriately. However mutual exploration ("playing doctor") is cause for alarm, rather than your choosing just to distract and educate, when any child is being exploited by another: forced participation or when an older child is involved. Your swift intervention is not only appropriate at that time, it is <u>mandatory</u>.

Very often, parents respond to such a situation with remarks such as:

- "Well, you should have run."
- "You shouldn't have been playing with him/her in the first place."

- "Why were you kids taking off your clothes, anyway?"

These responses, while being typical reactions, are not what any child needs following an incident of exploitation or poor judgment. Admonishment is another way of blaming the victim and, therefore, teaches children that parents cannot be counted on as safe havens during times of difficulty.

When parents are visibly upset after such encounters, children immediately conclude that they have been "bad" and have caused Mommy and Daddy to be angry or distressed. If we have those feelings, we need to put them temporarily on hold so that we can engage our parenting skills to meet our child's needs following a serious, personal violation. A nurturing environment where healing can take place is of the utmost importance at this time. This is when children should be given the messages that they were not to blame, and that you are so glad that they were wise enough to come and tell you about the incident(s), so that you can help them avoid future abuse. Afterwards, when your child is not around, discuss your feelings and reactions with your spouse or some other empathic adult who can help you with your own sense of anger, frustration, and violation.

As any other activity which involves our bodies and sense of privacy, no child should ever be bullied into a situation which makes him/her uncomfortable. If this ever occurs, follow your instincts to protect the child who appears to be a victim of force, abuse, or intimidation. Children must be removed from such situations, and it's okay to discontinue the relationship with the abusive playmate.

Stay calm, direct, and firm. Commend your child for exhibiting distress or coming and telling you. Praise validates your child's response to his/her basic instincts: "This is not a good situation for me, and I don't like it. I want it to end. I need help." Your response also reinforces that you care about the child's feelings, and that you are a person who can help children to remain safe.

Funny names for funny places

Because preschoolers have more exposure to other children, they learn additional words for body parts and functions. So slang words, like "boobs" and "poopie," will enter the conversation from time to time. That's okay, and I urge parents not to get concerned lest they again reveal a preoccupation with sexual and elimination functions. A good idea is to remind a child that "boobs are really called breasts," but you don't have to do that every time. Kids like to experiment with the various words, and oftentimes the new words they learn or invent are much funnier, so it's a game to be using them.

The Canadian folk singer, Raffi, whose humorous and sensitive songs are loved by children of every age, everywhere, is a great example of someone who can take ordinary objects with everyday names and create hilarious new names which make us all laugh. Kids do that too. I have yet to meet a little boy who didn't think "hot dog" was a pretty silly name for a penis, and his laughter reveals his delight. No problem. If you continue to use the correct terms you have done your work. The important thing is that (s)he knows the right names and can use them.

Nude Dudes

I continue to believe that nudity at home when family members are bathing and dressing is perfectly natural. Small children usually like to be around their parents at a time when the parents are performing rituals which take little thought because parents are mentally available to chat. So, as long as you are comfortable and your child appears so, too, family nudity is not a problem.

However, if any member is <u>ever</u> ill at ease being nude or being around someone else who is undressed, then the nudity should end. Healthy people respect each others' feelings without being emotionally wounded, personally threatened, and without making others feel peculiar.

Using the commode is similar to nudity. Many parents and children share the bathroom while one of them urinates. At some point, either the adult or child may begin to feel less comfortable with these arrangements (usually around a child of the opposite sex) and will gradually seek more privacy. Many children of the same gender as the parent remain comfortable with nudity and bathroom sharing in each others' presence through adulthood. Nudity and bathroom sharing are not big issues in most houses; they are small, everyday life events which run their own course.

What these things are really about is our being in tune and respectful of our own preferences and feelings and those of our children. They are equally important. It is up to the parents to be sensitive to the nonverbal ways a child may communicate his/her discomfort. Remember that, until well into the teen years, children do not have the faculties to communicate about their feelings the way we adults can.

Kids depend more on physical behaviors, so it is up to us to pick up on their nonverbal cues.

"No" is a wonderful word.

Another area where this acceptance of children's feelings is really important and so frequently overlooked is in displays of affection. Many of us, somehow, have this distorted belief that children are being "good" when they give hugs and kisses to individuals we choose. Hugs and kisses are about affection, and affection is about our feelings. I want to choose the people to whom I will give my physical affection; that is part of maintaining my integrity. It is part of my self-care. I would resent having someone else's affection expectation imposed upon me. So please, respect that in your child as well. Sure, Aunt Elizabeth or Uncle Bob may feel hurt that your little Michael or Stephanie doesn't want to give a kiss. But what about Michael's and Stephanie's feelings?

If we are going to teach our preschoolers that they should put aside their reluctance about expressing affection so that somebody else will be satisfied, how do you think they will transfer that message years later at seventeen? Whose feelings do you think we will have taught them to worry about when they prefer not to engage in progressively more intimate sexual touching, after years of learning that "nice" boys and girls are responsible for other people's happiness? How prepared will they be when the leaders of their social group pressure them to snort a little cocaine, but our kids aren't equipped to be confident about their right to say "no thanks"? Think about it.

This issue, respecting and encouraging your child's right to determine who (s)he will and will not touch, is at the core of protecting your child against sexual abuse. Many of us have been instructed to discuss with our children certain typical situations where sexual abuse might occur. Unfortunately, there is no possible way that we can cover every likely setting for this grotesque offense against children. We also need to recognize that what makes this task especially challenging is that most abusers are adults whom we and our children know, respect, trust, and even love.

What we can do, instead, is to teach children to listen to their instincts and to take active steps in order to care for themselves. This way we maximize their ability to deal with threatening situations and reinforce that all-important message: "You are a bright person who is capable of making good decisions. When you don't feel good about something, it's alright to say 'no'."

Here is a true example of how children, in their literal way of thinking, cannot distinguish between kissing someone they perceive as an authority deserving of respect (so his/her feelings won't be hurt) and letting some other adult fondle him/her:

> One woman reported being sexually abused repeatedly by a relative. At one point, she asked her mother (who was unaware of the abuse) if children must always do what adults tell them to do. Her mother told her "yes." Of course the mother was talking about the usual orderly obedience we think of between children and teachers, police officers, and other authority figures. She had no idea that her daughter was really asking whether or not

she had to let an adult touch her. The woman went on to explain that as a child, she was torn between her terror about the abuse and worrying (as she had been taught) about not hurting her relative's feelings.

This story is not at all unusual. Communicate in word and deed to your child that his/her body belongs only to him or her, and then let your child express that clearly when necessary. Similarly, children learn from us that we will accept their wishes not to cuddle or kiss others--no matter who it is. We can teach them other ways of being sociable, such as shaking hands, smiling, or standing up tall and saying: "Good morning, Mrs. Smith." And if an adult pleads with them and tries to make them feel (intentionally or not) as if they should comply ("Oh, please, give Auntie a little kiss, or I'll be so sad when I go back home"), we will be there to support our child, modeling an answer such as "I'm glad that you have enjoyed being with Stephanie. As you can see, she prefers to shake your hand as a gesture of friendship." No excuses, no lengthy explanations, just a statement of fact: Stephanie prefers shaking hands.

Later, tell Stephanie how pleased you are that she listened to her inner voice and did not kiss Mrs. Smith when she knew that she didn't want to. Reinforce the social skills she did demonstrate. Above all, let her know that you support and admire the ways you see her taking good care of herself while being thoughtful of others, and that you will always be there to support her.

Imitation, Discovery and Exploration

Preschoolers are neat. Their special stage is one to be enjoyed rather than waiting for them to grow to another, older stage. They inquire about everything, when we give them opportunities and try things which we traditionally consider "male" and "female". Lots of little girls try standing up at the toilet to urinate as boys do. And preschool boys usually love to play with their mothers' make-up. I have seen parents panic, figuring the kid is ready to appear in drag! Nonsense. He is playing just as he does with old clothing and modeling clay. Just about every boy and girl has a story about cutting a friend's, sibling's, or doll's hair. They observe adults in our unlimited roles, and they love pretending that they can be who we are and do what we do. Allow them to explore in a safe and encouraging environment.

This is the beginning of "trying on" behaviors and styles so that your child can come to create what is his/her unique, totally personal male or female sexuality. This, too, is a process which will continue for <u>decades</u>. If you can celebrate this developmental process with your child and resist the urge for him/her to "grow up" or fit a certain, preconceived mold of what it means to be a little boy or girl, you will have fewer hassles, better relationships, a happier child, and many golden memories.

A Few More Words...

Because it is an issue for children at every stage of development, a few comments about sexual exploitation are in order. A great deal is written in this book about affection between family members; this never includes any of the touching which we associate with sexual stimulation.

Healthy sexual relationships cannot occur between two people who are not on equal footing in terms of status and power. So there is no such thing as a "loving" adult who has a sexual relationship with a child.

Intimate kissing or hugging, touching a child's breasts, buttocks, inner thighs, vulva, penis, or encouraging/allowing a child to do so to you are all unacceptable and illegal. Such activities do not enhance family bonding, nor do they help children develop a strong sense of self-worth. Rather, they destroy the very fabric of children's self-esteem, teach children that they have no power or control over what happens to their bodies, and that no one can be trusted.

Children raised in homes where they are permitted to express their feelings and have those feelings validated, are much less likely to be the victims of such abuse. A child who knows that she can firmly tell any other human being "NO!" has more power than a child who believes that (s)he is at the mercy of an aggressor. And each of those children must be certain that they can confide in their parents, and that their parents will always help to keep those children safe. Such parents or caretakers communicate that they are sensitive to children's needs, no matter how subtly expressed, and that they would never dream of imposing their desire for gratification upon any child.

Chapter Six

YOUNG SCHOOL-AGE CHILDREN

> Riding along the interstate highway in their big Chevy Suburban, a family traveled west to Colorado. Mom was driving and chatting with Grandpa up front. Dad was taking in the scenery with their nine and six-year-old daughters in the back seat. While everyone else was talking about the mountains and cool summer breezes, the six-year-old asked: "Daddy, how come I see Mommy naked a lot, but I never see you naked?"

Ah yes, the questions have moved from biological parts and functions to why we do what we do. Welcome to the next stage of sexuality education.

If you have been open and relaxed with your child about human bodies, their functions, and questions about sexual matters, then you will find these years to be more of the same process. We add a new dimension, now, as the questions become a little more sophisticated. Sex will probably remain a now-and-then sort of subject, not something that is tops on their list of concerns. But as children absorb more of the messages from television and real characters, they will seek your assistance to create some order:

- "Why doesn't Sandra's daddy live with Sandra's family?"

- "I thought you had to be married to get a baby."
- "Why did that man on the television keep touching that lady, even though she told him not to?"
- "I heard you and Mommy yelling. Are you going to get a divorce like Anthony's parents?"
- "Are you and Daddy going to have any more babies?"

If the atmosphere is a receptive one in your house, and you have successfully communicated by word and deed that any subject is okay for discussion (not lectures), your children will continue asking you to help fill in the gaps. When they hear "four-letter-words" they will usually suspect that these words are somehow different; and if you are an approachable parent, they will ask you. When they hear news reports about rape, they will come to you to put that story into a perspective which they can understand.

Sometimes my son heard words in jokes or conversations at school. Unsure what they actually meant, he came home and asked me. I recall one afternoon when he asked, "Mom, what's a cunt?" I told him what the word meant, and I went on to calmly explain that cunt is not a friendly term, and that most women experience it as a hostile word. I wanted him to have a frame of reference beyond a simple association with part of a woman's anatomy. Finally, I told him how glad I am that he asks his dad or me when he isn't sure about something because we believe that he is entitled to accurate information. Lots of kids get their information from friends who don't have the facts straight, and we want him to be on top of things. These conversations are always comfortable for both of us, which means that (so far) he keeps coming back to us for more. I can tell that he feels respected, that he knows we recognize that he is smart and capable enough to have the inside scoop, and that we are not going to hide anything from him. This is a part of our parenting about which I feel very good.

So, as you can see, children are now beginning to seek more than simple biological and physiological information; they are beginning to want this information within the context of its meaning in relationships. This is really all about your values. If you remain at ease and convey that these are important and interesting questions which you think about, too, your kids will keep approaching you as a resource, and they will get a chance to be exposed to your ideas. They feel respected when they see that you want to talk about your ideas, observations, and experiences with them, just as you do with your friends.

As you visit with your child, don't be afraid to express opinions which are different from the socially popular ones. Your beliefs are very important, and your kids need to hear them. If you were suddenly transferred to a foreign country where smoking is still considered chic, you wouldn't shy from answering your child's questions and including your opinions and evidence that choosing to smoke is foolish. You would be honest with your child about your beliefs, even if they were contrary to the socially current ones around him/her. You would probably want your child to consider why some individuals, especially adolescents, are attracted to cigarette smoking.

Sex is an important subject about which you have deeply-felt opinions to which your children deserve to be exposed. Your values may not be in agreement with those most frequently portrayed on the news or espoused at school, but your kids need to hear them. That's why you are such an essential component in your child's sexuality education. You are the individual who is willing to be totally honest, who cares deeply about his/her happiness and growth, and who has no political or financial motive.

For example, when a child mentions that an unmarried television character has a baby, this would be a time for a parent who does not view that situation as ideal to say something like: "Yes, she has, and I can see that she's working very hard to do a good job. Daddy and I are glad we waited to have our children until after we were married because we think it's important for children to have the benefit of both a mom and a dad." An unmarried parent will probably express a different viewpoint to his/her child about pregnancy and parenting without a committed partner. Or a parent might personalize the discussion with shared observations about someone the child and parent know, considering the factors which contribute and detract from a fertile environment for a child's development. Then see if your child wants to proceed from there or let it go for now.

With young school children, you will bore them if you get into deeper philosophical discussions than they are ready to consider. Parents need to stay at a more elementary level. Listen to your child for cues: Is this a request for facts? Is (s)he hoping to elicit your opinions?

If you're just getting started...

If you have been intimidated or shy about this part of parenting, about our bodies and their functions, if you have ignored their questions or given them storybook answers, it's time to bring order to this area of their development. If this is a frightening or offensive proposal to you, try to determine if there is something in your history which contributes to these strong feelings you are having. Understanding that part of your personal history and taking steps to overcome such roadblocks can be useful to you individually and as you embark on this aspect of parenting. What is essential here is that your impediments not interfere with your child's need to grow and understand.

If you've just delayed the onset of your open communication, hoping to extend your child's childhood, delay no longer. Rather than confusing the issue further with explanations about why you didn't give your kids straight answers to their questions, just begin with the first opportunities that present themselves. Your kids may have caught on to your evasive answers in the past and may no longer come to you with their questions and comments. If that's the case, look for opportunities, just as you would with a younger child (See the chapter about preschoolers). Start conversations with openers which encourage discussion:

- "Have you ever noticed ...";
- "When I was about your age I wondered about ...";
- "There's been a lot on television about _____ lately, and I'll bet you've been wondering..."; and
- "What do you think about _____?".

Your child wants and needs more information, and you are his best source. Look within you and around you for answers. Parents whose children are the same ages as yours or older are valuable resources. These are the workers in the trenches who are dealing with the same issues you encounter. Remember, too, that we are raising our children at a time that offers a wealth of information in books for various ages and stages of development.

Looking to others and to published materials for help with ideas and answers should not be considered as a suggestion to give your child a book about sexuality with the invitation: "Come to me if you have any questions." Not only is such an approach not good enough, it is foolish. What would an intelligent parent say about a teacher who handed his/her child an arithmetic text with the remarks: "Read this, and let me know if you have any questions."?

Learning about sexuality is not merely getting the "facts of life" straight in one's mind as though preparing for a multiple choice exam. Sexuality is about being male and being female. How we express that with our genitals is just one part of our sexuality. That's the area we have the most difficulty teaching, usually because it was not too artfully taught to us. We all learn about our sexuality as we watch and interact with others and as those individuals who are close to us reveal the meanings that they assign to life events.

Keep in mind that how you deal with life on a day-to-day basis is your child's primary source of information about what it means to be a man or a woman. How you interact with your child communicates what kind of respect you have for him, his experiences, and his questions as well as what you expect from him in your relationship.

No book, class, seminar, or individual can possibly provide a complete picture of human sexuality; it is a process with many contributing factors. What every parent must realize is that a very small portion of children's sexual socialization occurs during the conscious presentation of information and ideas. Kids acquire most of their attitudes about sexuality and relationships from their daily encounters and observations: TV, movies, older teen couples, peers, their parents' lives and relationships.

Again, savvy parents ask themselves: who are the TV and movie characters we invite into our child's world? What does our life tell our child about who we are and his/her importance in our world? In what way is our lifestye <u>today</u> enhancing our child's ability to love, value, and care for herself now and in the future...including her sexual ecology?

Anybody seen a hug around here recently?

I think that during these early school-age years while children are forming more relationships outside of the family unit and are less physically needy of us, we oftentimes get out of the habit of touching them. Tender and <u>appropriate</u> touching is a powerful form of bonding among mammals. I urge you to make a priority of hugging your kids and cuddling with them in ways that are comfortable for both of you. Believe me, kids will let you know what they don't like. That's a sign of an emotionally healthy individual--being confident in expressing likes and dislikes and setting personal boundaries. If you and your children have become physically distanced, this will need to be a gradual process. Kids are similar to adults; they rarely like immediate intimacy, especially if closeness is part of someone else's agenda.

In one house, their reading time is when they frequently cuddle on the couch. The mom also makes a point of getting up and hugging her kids and putting an arm around them when they come into the house after being out for the day. That's when she tries to drop everything and just listen. At the beach, they massage each other's feet or each others' shoulders after a long day of sun. Their kids have always liked it when either of the parents knocks on their doors as they read in bed before turning out the lights.

Many evenings, the mother sits on the side of the bed, and they chat. She says that they hold hands or squeeze each other's arms as little hugs. Sometimes, one child at a time, she massages their scalps as they close their eyes and relax, preparing for sleep. Bedtime is a great time for one-on-one sharing and developing close feelings between parents and children.

Many of these forms of touching are like the ones we do with our partners. This kind of "good touching" doesn't have to be reserved only for people who are sexual partners. Everybody needs affection. In our culture we have a strong tendency to discontinue touching from the time children are school-age until they somehow become eligible for it again with a sexual partner. Is it possible that this form of tactile starvation is a very real contributor to premature sexual experimentation, that our children are desperate for affection?

Our skin is the largest organ of the body and needs physical stimulation for us to feel emotionally good. Part of what children are looking for in their sexual involvement is being held. That sounds so simple when teen sexuality is seemingly such a complicated issue. But in a very real way, through our behavior, we demonstrate that cuddling within families is for caretakers and their small children. Other than that, it is for people who are romantically involved. Hence, in this culture, platonic friends do not walk down the street arm in arm (as they do in other cultures throughout the world), and parents and children get out of the habit of touching and being touched. So when the hormones start churning during the teen years, and they are already starved for physical affection, teens follow the unspoken rule of society: the need for affection is satisfied by someone to whom one is sexually or romantically attracted. This limited formula is a recipe for disasters.

I have seen families who have altered that societal rule by extending family affection beyond the toddler and preschool years. This is no guaranteed insurance policy against early sexual experimentation, but it does enhance family bonding, and helps members learn how to get their normal physical needs met in a healthful way that is appropriate to their stage in life and without putting them at risk. I haven't a statistic to wave as proof, but my common sense and observations tell me that regular, satisfying affection serves as a sort of governor, both balancing our sexual drive and sensitizing us to other forms of stimulation-- an absolute win-win formula.

I have encountered so many teenagers who talk about not wanting intercourse but wanting to be held and cuddled. This need for affection and love is unbelievably strong. So they reluctantly engage in sexual intercourse in order to get the affection they crave. Possibly, our gradual withdrawal of affection from our children is an unintentional set-up: we starve them, thereby forcing them to turn to others who are equally hungry for touching.

The early school-age years are the stage when children and parents become very busy with separate activities, longer school days, and after-school interests. All of that, followed by evenings of television and homework, leave little time for snuggling next to each other on the couch. If you can't make time to sit quietly together, look for other opportunities to touch and attend to each other:

- an arm around a shoulder while visiting;
- a gentle, loving squeeze of an arm while having a friendly conversation in the car;
- stopping into his/her room before going to bed with some affectionate words and a hug;
- a gesture after the two of you have completed a task together (teammates do it all the time).

Hang onto this important link with your children. It's a vital one in the human experience, and it's difficult to reclaim once missing from your relationship. After all, we cuddle our pets no matter how old they are; why not our children who have grown beyond the baby stage?

A continuing need to be heard

In the previous chapter, we talked about respecting a child's right to express (and not to express) affection when (s)he wants to and with whom. This is an avenue for self-responsibility and confidence-building.

Honest self-expression should not be limited to the area of affection. Starting with the preschool years and really gaining momentum during the early school-age years, children experience a growing need to express their preferences and feelings and to have that communication respected. Children who get regular experience stating their feelings without fear of punishment or belittling exit their front doors with active skills for protecting themselves. They have learned and experienced the success of telling other people that they have personal boundaries which they do not want others to overstep. They gain these experiences first at home as their expressed wishes and feelings are met with respect:

- "I don't want to give Mrs. Wrinkle a kiss."

- "I want to wear the dotted shirt with the plaid shorts."
- "I don't want to drink anything with my meal."
- "I don't like wearing that dress; it scratches my skin."
- "I don't want to take a bath with Jamie anymore. I want to bathe by myself."
- "I want to wear my panties to bed. My bottom feels better."
- "I like the door closed to my room and for you to knock before coming in."

Each of the above is about a child's body and personal space. So what if your kid's clothes don't match? It won't be the end of the world. But the experience of having stated her wishes about <u>her</u> clothing and having them honored is a major part of learning that she has a <u>right</u> to state her wishes in a polite manner. While we cannot always accommodate our children's wishes (What if she wants to wear the dotted shirt and striped shorts to the wedding where she has agreed to be the flower girl?), we can tell them that we <u>understand their feelings</u> and make efforts to accommodate them when possible. They also learn in such instances, that we don't always get to do exactly as we wish. All choices involve trade-offs: "If I want to be the flower girl, shorts and a t-shirt are not among the clothing options."

I do not suggest that small children be placed in charge of their own lives. Such a move would be virtual abandonment. Children, as do adults, need clear boundaries which help them to feel secure, loved, and guided. To raise children without limits is unrealistic, as life is filled with limits to insure a more orderly society. What I do suggest is that children always be given the space to voice their preferences in clear, polite terms without fear of chastisement or belittling. Once they have made their thoughts known, it is the exchange between the two of you and what <u>you</u> choose to do with the messages you are receiving from them which sets the stage.

Power in Process: Becoming a Responsible Person

The next step, after making room for honest self-expression, is for parents to listen carefully and determine "Who's territory is this?" All too often, we get caught up making six-year-old decisions, which the six-year-old ought to be handling. Such interfering disrupts a child's emotional, social, and even intellectual progress. For example:

- what to wear. This is usually about coats and sweaters. Most kids learn from the discomfort of being cold or wet to take responsibility for their own comfort and protection from the elements. And oftentimes kids are not chilled when adults are, usually because they are moving their bodies and generating their own heat.

- whether or not to eat dinner or how much to eat. I have yet to meet a child who is malnourished from a missed meal. If she doesn't get a bail-out in the way of a snack to "tide her over," she will learn without a lecture that it makes sense to eat while the chow is on.

- how they will spend their personal money. "What, out of money, and you want to buy a new building set? Yes, I'll bet you're disappointed; I am, too, when I've spent all of my money and want to buy a new outfit."

Practice in decision making, which involves many mental skills such as planning and logic, empowers a child, building her sense of confidence. It is <u>active</u> learning, and it offers occasions to celebrate a job well done and opportunities to create order out of errors. This is what self-reliance is all about.

The ongoing practice of making age-appropriate choices and working out the results of those choices without parental bail-outs means that, when children are teens, they have some real-life experiences with decision-making, not second-hand reports from their parents. That means that they will be better prepared to make responsible decisions when the stakes are much higher because they truly will understand how life works. Likewise, they know the exhilaration that comes from creating successes, and they want more of that.

A trick that I have learned (and for which I am deeply indebted to the Cline-Fay Institute in Evergreen, Colorado) is to give young children a couple of choices which I am "willing to live with." So I might say:

- "Do you want to play miniature golf or go see a movie?"
- "Shall we bake cookies or muffins this morning?"
- "Shall we walk or ride our bikes to the park?"
- "Do you want to wear your jacket or carry it?"
- "Do you want to do your homework before or after dinner?"
- "Do you want to clean your room now or before your next meal?"

The important thing is that they are getting actual practice making choices, experiencing the results of their decisions, and learning what works and what doesn't within their society. And they are doing this at a level which is manageable for their ages and stages of development. They find out that life is filled with trade-offs, and that sometimes that which seemed to be a great choice works out and at other times is disappointing.

These lessons not only help them learn much more quickly than any of our nagging, directives, or lectures, they also reinforce life's lesson that ultimately each of us is responsible for the choices we make. We parents are there as empathic consultants, and our children learn that they can come to us as they work through consequences that are different than those they had hoped would result from their decisions. Children feel very empowered when the authority figures in their lives trust them and view them as capable people.

How is this all related to sexuality? Because our sexuality is about who we are as individuals, anything which contributes to our functioning at a more competent level automatically enhances our positive sense of self and, therefore, the choices we make as we interact with our world. In that specific area of sexual behavior, it is only logical that a child who learns to accept, and even enjoy, responsibility for his actions at five or seven-years-of-age, will someday be a teenager (and later an adult) capable of more responsible sexual decision-making. He will have more experience with poor choices as well as workable ones, making him a better-qualified analyst of the choices before him.

This empowerment of your child is a continuation of the efforts from the infant and preschool years when you taught him about his body, its remarkable functions, and its care. Now there are the added twists about <u>why</u> people behave the way they do and how those issues relate to healthful living. Your child learns gradually about the reality that our decisions are not made in isolation, that they affect our happiness and that of those around us. This is the gradual and challenging task of doing what we can to raise responsible and capable children.

It is a daily learning to appreciate and accept oneself and others, to learn to be responsible for oneself and to others in the human community, to find the avenues which lead to happy living.

For now, what we can do is to be positive models about real life, its challenges, thrills, and its disappointments. We can start letting our children sample real life in ways which give their experiences and, therefore, their lives meaning. Our children will not be spared disappointments, so our parenting needs to include allowing our small children to experience <u>and</u> cope with small children's frustrations. "Protecting" them from hurt stunts their progress so that when they encounter teenage or adult disappointments, they are ill-equipped, even powerless, and, oftentimes, devastated.

An unusually wise elementary school teacher once told each parent with whom she had a conference: "Let your child struggle." That theme is regularly repeated by older parents who write letters to advice columnists, lamenting their own indulgences of their now-grown children. Generous parental love gives children the necessary space to gradually build the emotional, spiritual, intellectual, and physical muscles they will need to become capable and confident.

Through our presence, acceptance of our children and their feelings and moods, affirmations and physical touching, we can let them experience our unconditional love and support. We can answer their questions with direct responses that make them feel secure, rather than fearful and uptight about what lies ahead. Again, this costs nothing or little, it's about being there as models, listeners, and helpers so that they can develop their maleness, their femaleness, so that they can become fully integrated and <u>responsible</u> sexual beings.

Chapter Seven
PRETEENS

Most preteens still have a strong link with their parents and other authority figures who deserve their respect. They are very much a mixture of child and teen, at one moment asking to go to a rock concert and the next wanting to be "tucked in" at night. Kids this age exhibit tremendous creativity and playfulness while also having the capacity to inquire about areas that are usually the domain of adult curiosity (e.g., racial tension, capital punishment, war).

While some of their behavior may be "adult-like" (whatever that means), there is no need to rush them. Remember, they are in <u>process</u>. Even though most of their friends at this time may be of the same sex, some children will have opposite-sex friends with whom they work on special projects, go to movies, share athletic interests, etc. Let those relationships be, and please don't start teasing your child about his "date" or "girlfriend." I see kids become so resentful when the nature of their friendships is distorted that they terminate a valued relationship in order to put an end to the teasing which they perceive to be harassment. I think those kids have been robbed of special experiences.

I have read that makeup is one of the new growth industries targeted at the preteen age group. This is another example of accelerating the developmental stages, thrusting children into adulthood before they have had time to complete the work of childhood. David Elkind, the insightful author of those excellent books, <u>The Hurried Child</u> and <u>All</u>

Grown Up With No Place to Go, points out that we have removed our children's rights of passage and pushed them into adult symbols and behaviors before they are emotionally and cognitively ready. As a result, they experience tremendous and unnecessary confusion. At one moment they appear and are treated as young adults, and at the next moment, they are being told what to do as if they were (because they are) still children.

You may find yourself facing the situation where the pressure is intense for your daughter to wear makeup and clothing which you believe are inappropriate. I thought that a friend of mine handled this so well when she and her daughter encountered it. She called a makeup consultant at a store and explained the situation: young daughter asking for makeup yet mother wanting to minimize its use while being sensitive to the social pressures. They arranged an appointment, and the beauty consultant focused on the daughter's healthy skin as a tremendous asset, suggested some cleaning potions, a little powder, and an eyebrow brush. The daughter left her appointment delighted that she now had the right equipment to carry in her purse, knowing more about how to look attractive among her peers, and feeling beautiful.

- The mother and daughter avoided a stand-off.
- The daughter felt that her wishes had been heard and validated.
- The mother had prevented her daughter from being pushed too fast and too far, yet had worked within the social setting, which was part of her daughter's support network.
- The mother accepted the fact that on this matter her daughter was more receptive to

some other adult's opinion (the beauty consultant).

The demands you face from your preteen, and later from your teen, will depend upon your area of the country and the fads that are unique to your child's group. So there are no dependable rules and traditions in the way our grandparents just knew when it was time that a boy got to move from knickers to long trousers. You will have to use your own judgment. Here, too, I believe that being a parent who works with his/her child to clarify these issues in relation to a child's feelings and long-term goals is being that wise friend, that consultant, that your child needs now.

Start Talking Before They Start Changing.

If you have not yet talked about the ways girls' and boys' bodies change, it is time to get busy. When we can talk about these things <u>before</u> the changes start occurring, we feel less awkward and so do our kids. They are becoming increasingly sensitive about their bodies and do not want the focus of such conversations to be so obviously about them. For example, little girls who grow up knowing that their mothers menstruate, seeing pads and tampons, and understanding their use will not be alarmed as they might be if they are suddenly informed of imminent physiological changes. A growing girl's regular observations of her mother's experiences give the daughter a frame of reference in which to understand menstruation as part of becoming physically mature.

Same with boys. If their questions have been answered as they have been asked, with additional information provided along the way, they already know that, pretty soon, they will be experiencing secondary hair growth and wet dreams. Prior to the preteen stage, they will have wanted to know how the "seed gets inside the mommy." That is when they first started learning about arousal, ejaculation, semen, and sperm. Those discussions were the opportunities for parents to say things like: "In a few years, when your body starts changing like your cousin Robert's has, your genitals will get larger and when you have erections, sometimes during the night, you'll have ejaculations even though you aren't having sex..." Now the changes are nearing, and the need for a clearer understanding is pressing. It is useful to all participants if there is a history of comfortable inquiries and answers about sexual matters. When that is the case, these conversations, as puberty nears, are so much easier for everyone.

If you want to introduce this subject to a preteen and have not had much discussion to date, you will fare better if you remain casual about it so (s)he is neither alarmed nor embarrassed. Especially if you have avoided discussing sex until now, I think that rather than being uncharacteristically coy in your introduction, it is much better to be direct and say something along the lines of: "Jim, I've been delaying talking to you about anything related to sex because I've been feeling kind of uncomfortable discussing it with you. I'm not sure why I've felt this way. After all, sex is just another normal part of life. Anyway, I think it's better to start talking, now, than to continue ignoring sex." Then begin with body changes or a personal experience; see how much he knows, and build gradually. Just make sure that you don't drop the subject after this one conversation. Correct the mistake of having neglected sexuality discussions by bringing it into your lives as a regular topic whenever anything about sex, relationships, STDs, pregnancy, or any other related subject surfaces.

You can count on your child being curious; now you want him/her to be aware and comfortable with the changes that he/she will experience. If you have included sexual matters in previous conversations, now you might want to say things like: "Have you noticed that any of the girls in your class have started growing breasts? Which of the guys' bodies are starting to change?..." Or if you notice that your daughter's breasts are starting to develop, it's fine to say: "Gee, I see that you're starting to grow breasts. Your body is beginning to change. As it continues to change, you'll be getting menstrual periods too..." You might mention that some girls are eager to wear bras while others prefer to wait until their breasts grow noticeably larger. Either way, you want your daughter to know that she can go purchase some or you'll help her, that you want to do this on her timetable. This is all so much easier for both of you if you are casual about your own body as a parent.

There are certain things that all healthy male and female bodies do. Let your kids know about these normal functions and the changes that they will experience as they develop, including the fluctuating moods which accompany hormonal changes. Use the correct terms so that they know words like menstruation, periods, erections, ejaculation, nocturnal emissions, and wet dreams. It's okay to mention other terms like "hard-on," "boner," and "jack-off." If we sound overly technical or only speak of sexuality as "sacred," they surely aren't going to come to us for facts and reflections. Our demeanor will have told them that we don't know anything about "real" emotions and experiences, and that we lost our senses of humor at the end of the Dark Ages.

Some people prefer to hand their kids a book about puberty and sexual behavior, tell them to read it, and instruct the kids to come with questions if they have any. They don't isolate any other subject that way, and I can almost guarantee that most kids won't bother coming around with questions, at least not their <u>real</u> questions. It's just too weird.

Learning about our sexuality is a process of learning who we are and our various ways of expressing ourselves. It does not come from reading one book or a particular article. Nor do we suddenly have a sexual identity because of one or two talks we have had with our parents or some other expert. Our sexuality develops gradually, evolving over a lifetime. So please keep talking about feelings, changes, ideas, preferences, everything. So long as your children know that this subject is as appropriate in your house as discussing the new model cars, and that people vary in their opinions while still respecting and loving each other, you will be on a very solid path.

What's especially important during these preteen years is that they understand how their bodies will change, that they know that the changes are normal, that they are aware that this is a process of development, both physical and emotional, and that <u>it</u> <u>is</u> <u>good</u>. Complement all of that with parents who are receptive to talking about <u>how</u> these bodies and the feelings inside of them relate to happy living, and you and your kids will have the best of family sexuality education.

Should we talk about family planning?

Although every parent hopes that his/her child will delay intercourse until much later, family planning should be included in these on-going discussions about sex. Do not assign this to a one-time, sit-down session in your house to review all of the forms of family planning. Rather, include information about the various methods on an on-going basis. Here is an example which happened recently:

My preteen daughter and I drove by the county hospital in our area, where many very young mothers and small children were crossing the street. We had just been by the office of a colleague who works with pregnant and parenting adolescent girls and their children. I told my daughter a little about my friend's work, which was a natural entree for us to talk about teens and family planning. We talked about birth control pills, the physical side-effects experienced by many women who take them, and the fact that the birth control pill does <u>not</u> provide protection against STDs (sexually transmitted diseases). That brought us to condoms and spermicides.

Because she didn't know about spermicides, we talked about insecticides and considered what the root words and suffixes told us, so that she concluded that "spermicides kill sperm." Bingo! We didn't cover every aspect of those three, individual methods or combinations, but we got started. And it occurred within the context of real people in a real setting: the young mothers leaving the clinic at the county hospital.

A recent morning newspaper had a big article about the startling rise of antibiotic-resistant STDs, yet another entree to a discussion--right here in our own kitchen. The opportunities are everywhere; parents just need to make all aspects of sexuality education a priority so the conversations are as regular as discussing sports.

What about masturbation?

I find that when I work with parents, there is tremendous relief when I mention this topic, and they appreciate my talking about the way we have addressed it in our house: openly and very honestly. The subject of erections first came up (no pun intended; I caught this one in the editing, and it's just too perfect to erase) one night when I was having a tuck-in chat with one of the children and was asked: "Mom, what's a boner?" As I answered his question about "boners," we talked about what happens when boys and men have erections. So I explained masturbation and told my child that masturbation is one way that lots of people deal with arousal, experience sexual pleasure, and become more aware of and comfortable with their bodies' sensitivities. I talked about it feeling good and about it being an appropriate way for people to deal with their sexual desires when they are not in long-term, committed relationships and not prepared to assume the responsibilities for a baby.

I have worked with enough people who have felt tremendous shame about themselves because at some point, someone told them that masturbation is dirty and/or sinful. I have never heard or read a convincing argument against masturbation. In fact, I believe that it is a very normal sexual activity:

- It helps an individual address sexual arousal in a responsible manner when sexual intimacy with another is not yet appropriate.
- It can be a relaxed opportunity for boys and girls, men and women to become sensitized to what does and does not pleasure them.

● It can be an experience which gives girls and boys positive feelings about sexual excitement and orgasm.

● It is okay for those who choose to, and it's okay if people choose not to masturbate.

● Masturbation cannot make a baby, and it does not spread sexually transmitted diseases (STDs).

Because there are still a lot of different stories out there about masturbation, talk to your child about it. Let them know that it's okay, that it isn't deviant, and that bad things don't happen because people masturbate. Again, a holistic approach to our bodies applies here; if we can self-pleasure other parts of our bodies, why not our genitals?

Physical Maturation is Not a Competitive Sport.

Just as masturbation is an individual thing, so, too, are children's rates of change in physical and emotional development. By now, all kids realize that not everybody likes the same foods, excels at the same sports and school subjects, has the same body shape, etc. So as this process of growing into an adolescent continues, from time-to-time it's nice for them to be reminded that sexual maturation occurs at different times in different people.

Our children know a dear friend of ours, a big, hairy man with a thick beard and deep voice. They were surprised to learn that this man was still a small, boyish fellow his last year of high school. He experienced a rapid physical development during his first two years of college. Another man they know started maturing during his junior year in high school, three years <u>after</u> his younger brother! I was always the tallest in my class and felt awkward about being physically mature before my girlfriends. It helps children so much to know that their experiences are "normal" and to know that "normal" has a pretty broad range. One of the best ways that we can communicate our understanding of what they are going through and reassure them about their own development is to share with them our own experiences and recollections from that time.

Vital Support Networks

Peer relationships are also important in this process of getting comfortable with themselves as they change. Through various friendships, they can discern that everybody is changing in their own individual ways. Allow your children to participate in group activities with other kids their ages if they indicate interest or if you learn of a group which might interest them. Whether it's your church/temple youth groups, scouting, or other groups which encourage cooperative projects, <u>belonging</u> to a group of peers is an important part of the process of developing an identity--not for everyone, but for many. Working towards a common, identified goal with other individuals helps develop social skills and gives children's lives meaning.

Much has been written about the human need for purpose in life and the lack of that element in the lives of modern, Western children raised in non-agrarian societies where they are not needed, only wanted. Being part of a group which enjoys cooperative activities contributes real meaning and a sense of belonging at a critical time in their development.

This is precisely what teen gangs are all about: group membership which gives kids some meaning and a sense of belonging. In these groups the kids themselves make decisions and perform the tasks necessary to the group's operations. The members must be alert, contributing participants to maintain status within the gang structure. A close look at gangs highlights why so many kids reject big, adult-financed, adult-led, and adult-operated activities which give the adults a sense of purpose as helpers and frustrate the kids still stuck in the role of helpees.

Group success depends upon every member's attendance, active and useful participation, and group decision-making, so that every member feels needed and valued.

Group activities at this age offer an abundance of new adventures in areas where your child might otherwise never get exposure--camping, sailing, astronomy, film making, community service, whatever. Many of us have heard adults comment that they first became interested in a particular area when an enthusiastic scout leader or faculty advisor took an interest in them and their work. In building new skills and developing new interests, young adults gain confidence in themselves, an added dimension to their developing sexuality (their maleness or femaleness). They carry this confidence into their other relationships, giving them still another advantage as they begin encountering more situations where they must make healthful decisions for themselves.

I think it's important for us to remember that studies in the area of adolescent sexual behavior have found a pattern between kids with goals and personal successes and the delayed onset of sexual (i.e., genital) activity. People who have a lot going for them and who have achievable plans for their futures are less inclined to risk their present and future happiness for temporary thrills. In fact, their present success almost always has come about because they have been willing to delay some gratification in order to get what they want. For adolescents, it is oftentimes delaying social gratification during the week (now), postponing it until the week-end (later), so that they can succeed in school (now) and get into the better universities (later). The point is, these adolescents who delay sexual involvements have hands-on experience with regular, satisfying activities. They possess the behavioral skills to delay some of their gratification and to select other ways of expressing their emerging sexuality.

You and group participants can help provide frameworks in which preteens and teenagers can experience successes and establish goals. This does not mean that kids have to stop dreaming and stay on track for every long-term goal that they imagine. What this means is that they have opportunities to flex their mental, physical, and emotional muscles to achieve something that is theirs by choice and which adds meaning to their lives. Some will choose to concentrate on Boy Scout Merit Badges. Others will want to become school newspaper editors, good jazz dancers, mechanics, or the best woodworkers and typists in their schools. Finding an area for accomplishment goes beyond "keeping busy"; we are talking about having meaning in one's work and relationships.

These activities with their peers also give kids a chance to bond with other kids, to feel close to others as a result of their unified efforts. Here, they will experience the sensation of being included, at times rejected, coping with disappointment and successes, sharing the secrets of their hearts, making more decisions that affect themselves and others, and being responsible. This is an important phase that offers some protection (unlike being out on their own) while they "test the waters"--trying on varied styles of maleness and femaleness, making comparisons between the styles they observe among their peers and the adults in their lives. Their group activities give them another arena in which to talk about the changes they are experiencing and to compare themselves and their feelings with others of their own age.

When teens talk about why they become sexually active, they give lots of reasons. Among those reasons are the same experiences that kids involved in fulfilling youth groups report enjoying: belonging, feeling close to others, feeling good about themselves, having someone really care about them. It doesn't take a wizard to figure out that experiencing these good feelings and fulfillment in group and other age-appropriate activities is a much better avenue than experiencing them through teen sexual intercourse.

The Parental Support Network: Letting Them Own Their Challenges

And what sort of belonging and fulfillment do they find in their relationships with us, their parents? The extent to which our children remain voluntarily close to us at this time will depend more upon us than upon them. And for those children who have a parent who is their friend as well as mentor, they have the gift of wisdom and insights (not lectures) which their peers cannot yet give them.

If you want to be this person, continue the path of being a good listener and guide, not a dictator. Allow your children to develop by respecting what they have to say, reflecting their feelings back to them, permitting them to make choices that preteens should make, and to experience the consequences (the challenging as well as the easy) of those decisions. When they get into binds, be there for consultation if they ask for your ideas; but communicate your respect for them by allowing them to solve these preteen challenges which are the results of their choices.

As they enter adolescence, far too many children have no idea what it means to tackle the natural consequences of their decisions. Someone has always bailed them out so that they never experience disappointment and hurt. Is it any wonder that so many teenagers in the United States suffer from "magical thinking" when it comes to sexual behavior, drinking and driving, cheating on exams, and drug use? With no history of coping with the unpleasant results of some of their choices, they continue into the teen years thinking that they will never have to "face the music." When pregnancy and/or sexually transmitted diseases become part of their reality, no one can protect them from the tough reality of their situation. Having had little or no previous experience coping with little troubles, they are now playing in the big league, facing major, big-time trauma. It is inexcusable for us to keep them unprepared. While we parents may temporarily feel better when we intervene in their troubles, usually our efforts are actually <u>interferences</u> in their acquisition of life skills.

You can help increase the odds that your children will be spared the difficult circumstances of premature sexual activity by letting them make age-appropriate decisions and cope with real consequences <u>now</u>, getting acquainted with cause and effect. No need to lecture and threaten before they decide, nor to belittle and scold afterward. Life teaches its own lessons, and our lectures alienate us from our children. This sounds tough at first, but once you start respecting your child's right to these vital life lessons, you will find that you have fewer arguments and blaming sessions with your children. Actually, you will enjoy more exchanges that feel like those adults have when problem-solving with friends. This occurs when the parents are willing to keep their hands off of a challenge that rightfully belongs to their child. You will also find that they assume more responsibility for themselves and appreciate you more.

Here are just a few, very typical situations that preteens frequently encounter when they are repeatedly bailed out by their parents:

- Assignments left until the last minute. Parent drops everything, helps with research and typing. Lesson learned: People with servants don't need to be good time managers.

- Personal money is spent when kid gets an urge. When friends invite him/her for an activity, kid is broke. Parent doesn't want child to miss activity and makes a loan (of which everyone loses track) or just coughs up the cash. Lesson learned: People with generous bankers don't need to budget their money.

- Clothing is not put in the laundry. Child has "nothing to wear" at 5:30 p.m. Friday for a 7:00 p.m. function. Parent drops everything, grumbles about lack of planning, does washing and ironing. Lesson learned: "One hour Martinizing" is a twenty-four hour service, even if your parent's name isn't Martin.

What can parents do in such situations?

1. Empathize with the child's frustration due to lack of planning. This does not mean assigning blame, identifying the cause of the problem, or recommending how to solve the problem. It means communicating that you <u>understand</u> how he feels (e.g., frustrated, tense, angry) and letting him own this issue.

2. Never lecture. Lecturing takes the focus off of the kid and his situation and places it on you. In addition, you will probably be viewed as a jerk for nosing in on his business and acting like an authority. Lecturing is a no-win strategy for a parent in this situation. Besides, it represents the parent's unwillingness to let the child own the problem.

* Numbers 1 and 2 help your child view you as an <u>ally</u>.

3. Do not jump in to solve the problem or give unsolicited advice. Rather, what you might do is say something like: "I have an idea which might help you," or "I had a similar problem once." Then <u>wait</u> for your child to solicit that advice or information. If she doesn't ask for help, move to your own activity so that you will keep your nose out of this issue which <u>she</u> needs to resolve. She may need time to digest this challenge and may later come to you for advice.

4. If you are asked to help with a solution and your child moans: "Oh, that would never work," just say "Okay," and let it go; after all,

this is <u>your child's problem</u>. Let him/her own it. In such situations, kids usually get a strategy together pretty quickly and experience some of the more positive feelings that come from developing and implementing solutions to everyday problems. Even if they don't work it out and just walk about grumbling, that's part of their personal process for problem handling. Different from yours? Probably, but that's okay; you are demonstrating respect for their individuality and belief in their abilities to tackle life's challenges.

5.   Always stay pleasant. Remember, you aren't the one with the problem; and this is a very important learning event for your child. Does this damage their self-esteem? Does it ruin their sense of self if they can't work things out? No. The experience equips them to think more broadly and entertain more possibilities in other situations. These are common, everyday difficulties, and parents need to permit young children, as well as teens, to calmly learn the art of living, which includes dealing with challenges.

It is best not to warn children that they would be wise to be on their toes and consider all of the factors when making choices; they are learning this gradually in ways that are appropriate for their ages. Life has a great, natural way of teaching this lesson all on its own, day by day--if we'll just stay out of the way and let that happen. They are learning by doing and gaining self-respect in the process. All the while, they are supported by our love, interest, and willingness to be good listeners and friends.

We have oftentimes heard that experience is the best teacher. Let's not get in the way of our children's chances to become successful. Parents who truly believe that it is unloving to keep their children dependent upon them are satisfied with who they are as adults and are delighted with the progress they see their children making...one day at a time. In this process, the kids are becoming more responsible and confident about their abilities to manage their lives, while both parents and kids are becoming better friends.

We are trying to raise sexually healthy boys and girls who will be responsible and happy men and women. So be the very person you would want to consult, and you will be the friend and guide your child needs and deserves.

Getting A Discussion Started

If your family has little or no history of sharing opinions and feelings, you may find that when you try to solicit your preteen's thoughts so that you can discuss matters of human sexuality, the answer is "I dunno." That's okay, and you probably ought to expect such a reply. We know that a preteen or teen has some impressions, but perhaps he isn't yet ready to articulate them, especially if he has doubts about how well his opinions will be received.

For example, if in the past you have established yourself as the family or world authority and your opinion has been the opinion, your child might hesitate to differ with you--fearing ridicule, rejection, shame, whatever. This would be a good time to talk about your present willingness to accept that you don't have all of the answers, and that you are honestly curious about your child's ideas. Most kids (just like their parents) will need to see such an attitude demonstrated for a while before they are willing to take any risks. So you might expect your kid to inch into discussions very carefully. His past experiences have taught him that he will get burned if he disagrees with you. He must now have a pattern of positive experiences where you really do accept his right to have his own ideas and use the shared ideas as fuel for conversations rather than debates.

At times when you would like to get casual discussions going, and "I dunno" is the best response you get, you can improve your odds if you maintain the attitude that this is part of a really interesting and exciting process, not a critical life assignment. I have worked with a lot of kids and have found that, when a situation which is related to sexuality and relationships presents itself, it works best to draw out my kids' or students' thoughts before I share my own. Their ideas are important, and the group discussion can only succeed if everyone feels free to express an opinion. Open exchanges take place when the participants are confident that there is honest interest in them and their ideas, and that they will be treated respectfully. I try not to get critical or judgmental (e.g., "That was awful," or "He is so immoral."), finding it much more useful to ask questions which encourage analysis. When adults are judgmental, the kids know that there really can't be an open discussion and that they might be the next targets of judgment. A rigid approach stifles open discussion.

Later in the conversation, when my opinions and reactions are solicited, I have learned to talk about how I personally respond to the material or subject we're discussing and why. I speak in terms of personal experiences (mine and others I know or read about) and knowledge, and I leave room for others to comment about their reactions, which I assume may be different from my own. I attempt to create an atmosphere where they will be equally comfortable making contributions so that we can really start addressing the issues and how our choices impact our lives and those of others. The only difference between these conversations and our discussions about American military, trade, and immigration policies is the subject matter: sex.

Because the atmosphere makes it clear that everyone has permission to have her own feelings and thoughts, punishments (e.g., resentments, anger, ostracism) are not even a consideration. It is up to the adult who wants to get the discussion started to establish the informal and accepting ambience.

If you don't already have the implicit understanding that it is safe to reveal one's opinions, I suggest you not begin with a topic as sensitive and personal as sex. Talk about other current topics like public funding for art, U.S. military presence in other countries, or the management of American forests. After you have some positive experiences exchanging differing opinions in a friendly atmosphere, you will both feel more comfortable broaching a much more volatile subject: sex.

Informality is essential, too. If it is casual and you are asking someone for her opinion, just as you might ask if she prefers Coke or Pepsi, you are more likely to get an answer. If the format is formal and your child senses that you have "staged" it or that you are looking for the "right answer," again sex is getting segregated treatment, and you are less likely to stimulate discussion.

Let me give you a <u>very</u> casual, unplanned example which really occurred and which depicts what I am describing:

A friend of mine has a preteen son who had just finished eating dinner alone with his parents. Toward the end of dinner, the conversation somehow became focused on penis sizes, both erect and flaccid (perfectly normal concern for a preteen who is at the height of curiosity about his changing body). As the son was leaving, the mother lightly asked her son if he remembered which is the body's biggest sex organ. He laughed and said: "Sure, Mom, the mouth. No, I really do know; it's the brain." With that, he got up from the table patted his mother's shoulder, and the conversation ended on a humorous note.

I think this anecdote reveals several important things about this family and what is going on between the members:

- Sex is an acceptable topic for discussion, no different than talking about kidney sizes or lung capacity. So curiosity about sex is accepted, as is curiosity about all subjects.
- This family has a sense of humor, and they don't lose it when sex is the subject.
- Although the parents and child had never discussed oral sex before, the child exhibited some knowledge of it by his answer. I think that his remarks reveal that he has not been exposed to notions about genitals being dirty. Therefore, he did not have the automatic

reaction to genital-oral stimulation as being repulsive.

- Because the child and parents had not yet spoken of oral sex, the child had no knowledge of his parents' opinions about it; however an atmosphere already existed in the home which made him comfortable enough to mention it without any fear of being chastised or of offending or embarrassing his parents.

- Sex, as any other topic, may surface as the focus of conversation or as a tiny component.

This little scene will be repeated many times, just in different ways. It wasn't planned, and the subsequent ones probably won't be either. Sexual understanding is a life-long process, in this case occupying just a few minutes, and the above conversation was just one small part of that process. Because sex is a normal topic for discussion, neither the parents nor the child experience anxiety about when to talk about it or what to say. It is treated like any other subject of interest.

You see, you do not have to plan and fuss about getting the right materials together, the best setting, and contacting an "expert" before you talk to your children about sexual matters. Cues for conversations about sexual topics, from the most simple to the very complex, are all around us. What it does take is your willingness and ability (which you may have to develop) to create a safe and interesting atmosphere where the message is clear that we are all in the process of learning about life.

NOW WE'RE IN THE BIG LEAGUE

When children's mental processes and, therefore, their interests and behaviors start moving toward a more "teenage" level, the nature of discussions, observations, and behaviors in regard to sexuality will also move to a new level. While they will still want factual information (e.g., specifics about family planning, what happens during an abortion, in what kinds of sexual acts lesbians/gays engage, etc.), they will now be much more interested in placing those facts within a philosophical context.

They will not be content with basic information alone; they will want to know why some people believe that certain behaviors are immoral or unwise while others engage in them readily. For example, they may need help clarifying why their parents strongly disapprove of extra-marital relationships while the entire viewing audience was sympathetic to a movie couple, each of whom had a spouse who knew nothing of the new romance. They will be curious as to why some people believe that abortion is okay for certain reasons yet not for others. As a more immediate concern, they will want to consider how sexual choices enhance relationships and communicate honest love and how those same acts, in other instances, can also exploit. They will want to develop a deeper understanding of the nuances of sexual expressions and why some gestures are appropriate in some relationships while not in others.

As you can see, these are not "facts" which they are going to find in their school sex education textbooks. These are questions about values, our belief systems, and the expectations that people have about intimate relationships. They are the issues which make human sexuality such a challenging and exciting field for thought and study. If you are open to your child's questions and new ideas, you will find yourself questioning your own beliefs, sometimes changing them and, at other times, finding that these honest discussions have strengthened your convictions.

No matter the outcome, you are involved in a magnificent process of self-understanding. I have worked with middle school, high school, and college students for years, and I find this time of new awareness and inquiry to be fascinating. Somehow the subject of human sexuality takes us through every known emotion and can be an inspiring reminder of what awesome creatures we are.

I truly hope that you enjoy this stage of the journey with your children. In sharing more of who we are and who we are becoming, we create an ambience where kids and parents can start the process of being very special, adult friends.

Chapter Eight

USER-FRIENDLY PARENTS

Especially when your kids start getting older and they extend their sexual curiosity, their concerns will become more personalized and therefore more intense. They will grow in their awareness that in real life sexual choices involve trade-offs, and they will begin to experience these in the context of personal and pragmatic, emotional and physical urges and goals. Because they need us now as caring and insightful sounding boards, it is time to check ourselves out on the tolerance scale. You see, parents who want to be their children's primary source of information about sexuality will be successful only if they make a determined effort to be approachable, not only about sex but about any other subjects that are of importance to their children. The value of this principle (being approachable) increases as the children mature although, ideally, parents exhibit this characteristic from the start. Always remember, it is never too late to change your course; many parents have.

Tolerance, acceptance, and the willingness to entertain others' opinions in a relaxed manner develop slowly as we become comfortable with ourselves and others. These come to us when we acknowledge that good people can and do disagree at times, and that we are all in the process of unfolding our individuality. An essential ingredient in any quality relationship is the mutual belief that the other party is of good will.

Just for a moment, think about the individuals you find attractive in the sense of being comfortable approaching them with your ideas, feelings, and even your personal secrets. We are not inclined to take risks with people who will judge us harshly, laugh at us, make us feel foolish, or who are dogmatic. Rather, we are attracted to people who accept us as we are, who listen to us and consider our opinions and feelings, and who do not push their point of view on us. Such individuals stand a greater chance of influencing us because they have captured our emotional and intellectual attention, and they have conveyed respect for us.

Our children want this, too, but we oftentimes fail to provide such an environment because we think we will appear soft and thereby fail to get our important messages across to them. One of the problems with this belief is that we come across as narrow and insistent, and in the process they turn us off. No one wants to listen to an authority who will not listen in return. So now we do not even have their willingness to remain attentive and interested; we have lost the chance to translate our ideas and values.

Being accepting of our children and their beliefs, which may differ from our own, is not the same as abandoning our beliefs, nor pretending to approve of behavior or values which are contrary to our own. Acceptance means communicating to our children that we love and respect them, and that we are interested in their lives just because they are our children. In addition, it involves hearing what they have to say and remaining loving even when they do not agree with us. Some of the surest ways to close their minds to our ideas and values are forcing our opinions, getting upset and defensive, making negative remarks about them, and belittling their beliefs rather than calmly highlighting the life-enriching aspects of our own ideas.

Quite the opposite, the advantage of a receptive, friendly manner is that our children learn that it is safe to ask us questions and bounce new ideas off of us. We are "friendly" resources.

As we all know, rarely does any one of us immediately arrive at a final conclusion on any subject. We work our way through important issues, pondering the multitude of factors. In the process, we frequently change our minds about what we believe. Children, and especially teenagers, are in an acute period of curiosity and consideration. If we hope to influence the development of their value systems and their choices, we must present our ideas in an inviting manner. We must be attractive, inviting personalities. Our children will not consider us as useful sources if we send off the pejorative signals of judgment, negativism, dogmatism, and the like.

A hallmark of mental health is the ability to get along with people who have different beliefs, accepting diversity. Men and women who cannot tolerate others with different values, who read magazines and newspapers that reflect only their sanctioned points of view, and who are critical of people who disagree with them are generally viewed as rigid and unattractive; for they cannot love the person behind the ideas, no matter how loving and caring that individual may be.

Older children are especially intolerant of intolerance. They are not attracted to us when we are authoritative, when we dominate the conversation, when we fail to listen to their ideas and feelings, or when we preach. One young woman who wanted to talk to her mother about premarital sex met the distressed and urgent response: "Oh, but you <u>have</u> to be a virgin when you get married!" That was the extent of their conversation. The mother's agitation, fear, and insistence closed the subject.

The tragedy is that such events do several things. First of all, the child rejects the parent as a source of information. In the above example, the daughter does not want to upset her mother; nor does she want to lose her mother's approval and trust by indicating that she (the daughter) sees some positive value in premarital sex. The daughter has been told (by her mother's voice and statement) that she cannot explore this subject with her mother as a resource.

Another unfortunate result is that such parents lose their roles as teachers and confidants. Because the mother has demonstrated that she finds even consideration of an idea different from her own a frightening proposition, this mother has communicated that her daughter must go elsewhere for information and elucidation. Now her daughter will miss out on some very valuable considerations that the mother might have shared on this subject--thoughts that reflect the mother's value system rather than those of society at large.

Is this a "bad" mother? Of course not. She cares deeply and holds her beliefs firmly yet is unable to package them attractively. Teens do not have to listen to us, and they will not if the experience is unpleasant.

Children whose parents are intolerant of people with other ideas conclude that their parents' love for them is dependent upon being in agreement on all matters and that there is no patience with mistakes or differences. This takes us right back to having as friends (and now children) only those people who agree with us. It is very frightening to children to think that their parents' love might be withdrawn should a child act or believe contrary to the parents' wishes. Children are especially aware of their fallibility; and for kids who know that vengeance and rejection are guaranteed responses from those they need for support and guidance (their parents), mistakes in their futures are like land mines. Deep down within us, to feel good about ourselves, human beings must know that we are lovable and will be accepted just because we are. I'm told that's why we're human beings, not human "doings."

Journeying Together

Children are out there looking at this great big world as a place to explore. They are born with curiosity. Parents who are not afraid to explore with their children will enjoy adventure and friendship for a lifetime. These parents are healthy adults who are continuing the process of growth and understanding and who allow their own curiosity to flourish. These men and women view their children's questions and considerations as exciting evidence that their children are truly contemplating life's important issues. They know that these are the kids who have a better chance of making positive life choices rather than having someone else's choices imposed on them.

Let's look at three typical scenarios of conversations between a teenage girl, Emily, and her mother, Mrs. Smith. I think that they portray some common attitudes and reactions that both hinder and enhance open communication.

Scenario # 1

Emily: Mom, I miss Janet. She's just never around anymore since she's been getting so heavy with Todd.

Mrs. S: Do you think they're having sex?

Emily: I know they have a few times. And I'll bet they're doing it more now that they go over to her house so much after school.

Mrs. S: Well Janet is a smart girl, and I suppose she knows what she's doing.

Mrs. Smith didn't pick up on Emily's feelings of missing her friend and the sense of loss and, possibly, anger that has come with seeing so little of Janet recently. Also, Emily may be attempting to talk about premarital sex with her mom via a discussion about a friend rather than about herself. By asking Emily no questions, Mrs. Smith fails to learn more about Emily's ideas and beliefs. And finally, Mrs. Smith displays nonchalance about Janet's early sexual involvement. Emily might easily interpret her mother's reaction as indifference and decide that continuing the conversation isn't worth the effort in light of her Mom's apparent apathy. Mrs. Smith never entertains the idea with Emily that Janet's behavior may be a risky and even a destructive sexual choice.

This is an example of many missed opportunities, and teens can tell you that it happens all the time.

Scenario #2

Mrs. S: Emily, Janet hasn't been around much lately. How's she doing? Are you two mad at each other?

Emily: We're not fighting. It's just that, well, since she and Todd started getting so heavy and in love, she's with him all the time.

Mrs. S: Emily, do you think they're having sex?

Emily: Well, yeah, sometimes, but they're really in love.

Mrs. S: Janet is a bigger fool than I ever thought. Doesn't she know that she could get pregnant or that Todd might give her chlamydia, gonorrhea, or some other sexually transmitted disease? I knew she was no rocket scientist, but I didn't figure she'd start screwing around. What a shame. Keep your distance, Emily, or people will think you're trashy too.

Mrs. Smith has communicated several things to Emily:

- She disapproves of premarital sex.
- One risks pregnancy and sexually transmitted diseases when sexually active.

- Those whose behavior violates her values will be treated harshly (name-calling, ostracizing).
- Redeeming qualities will be readily overlooked if one behaves contrary to Mrs. Smith's values;
- Not only the behavior will be scrutinized, but the individual will be judged, too (implies that Janet is "trashy").
- Once a teen becomes "sexually active" there is no turning back.

What conclusions does Emily reach from this brief exchange?

- My mother is not a safe person with whom to discuss sensitive subjects (e.g., premarital sex, abortion, homosexuality). She makes absolute statements, and there appears to be no inclination to entertain other ideas for discussion.
- My mother will hate me/abandon me if I ever make a really big mistake (e.g., become pregnant) while growing up. Her love for me is dependent upon my behavior, not who I am.
- I better not tell her anything about my friends if she might disapprove, because she won't want me to be with them anymore.

The result, of course, is that the daughter will feel less secure about her mother's love and care, she will seek out others for guidance on subjects of major life consequences, and she will limit the information she shares with her mother about her friends, activities, thoughts, and feelings.

Scenario #3

Mrs. S: Emily, how's it going with Janet? I haven't seen her much lately. She doing okay? What's she up to?

Emily: Yea, she's okay. I don't see her much either now that she's spending so much time with Todd.

Mrs. S: Sounds like they're pretty serious? What do you think?

Emily: Yea, they go over to Janet's house every afternoon after school. She doesn't hang around much with us anymore.

Mrs. S: You must really miss your time together.

Emily: Yea, I do. We used to have so much fun together, but now it's Todd, Todd, Todd, and we never get to be together anymore.

Mrs. S: I'm sorry to hear that. I know she's important to you. You've been close for a long time. Maybe this thing with Todd will cool off pretty soon.

Emily: No, I don't think so!

Mrs. S: I know Janet's mom and dad aren't home after school. Are you worried about Janet getting too involved with Todd sexually?

Emily: Of course! I know they've done it already, so that's probably why they're always going over to her house alone.

Mrs. S: Oh. Well, when you're feeling close to a boyfriend or girlfriend, going over to your house when the parents aren't home would be pretty romantic, feeling like you're married or something. You don't seem to think Janet having sex with Todd is such a hot idea. Are you worried about her in addition to missing her?

Emily: Yes; that's what I meant. She could get pregnant or something.

The conversation in Scenario #3 is actually just getting started. What's important for our consideration, just now, is to see how the atmosphere for a comfortable give-and-take has been established. No one is threatened in this dialogue: Emily's feelings are validated (that Emily is missing her friend and is concerned about Janet), and her opinions and thoughts are solicited and respected by her mother. Mrs. Smith, if on her toes, will pick up not only on her daughter's sense of loss but on her desire to talk about teen sexuality.

Lots of "what if" kinds of questions can arise during such typical conversations:

- What if Janet is sexually involved with Todd? Then,

     how is their relationship affected?

     how does that impact Janet's other relationships (friends, parents, teachers, employers...)?

     might it have any impact on later relationships with boys and men? How?

     what kinds of communication skills are Janet and Todd likely to be developing? Are these any different from young couples who choose to express their love and caring in other ways?

- What if Janet were to get pregnant? Then,

     what if Janet had an abortion?

     what if Janet married Todd?

     what if Janet gives birth and relinquishes her baby for adoption?

     how might Todd be impacted by any of these decisions?

     what if Janet wanted to complete school (high school and, perhaps, university)?

As you can see, the possibilities are endless, depending upon the attitudes of the participants.

- Is this to be a session where a parent stuffs his/her ideas into the child? Or is this an opportunity for us to express thoughts, feelings, and beliefs that are important to us, to hear those of people we really value in our lives, and thereby grow closer?

● Will this be a springboard for investigating related topics (e.g., sexually transmitted diseases, family planning, abortion, homosexuality) together or at the library, church/temple, or a community organization?

● Are we able to address sex with the same calm and reason or, in this instance, will we again isolate it by becoming desperate and insistent for our children to buy our point of view?

Probably more so with sex than with any other topic we discuss with our kids, we parents set the mood. Remember, it is always all right to tell your child that you feel anxious about this subject, if you do. And it is okay for you to have strong beliefs, because savvy parents realize that our sexual choices can alter the course of our lives. Go ahead. Tell your children that because you love and respect them you want them to have the knowledge and understanding that you have on critical life matters (e.g., drinking and driving, sexual experimentation, college choices, the dynamics of relationships, tobacco use, eating disorders, etc.).

We have heard it over and over, and I have listened to it repeatedly in my work with students: kids want their parents to care about them, to make an investment in their children's lives, to talk about life with them. And as they grow older, they want their parents to speak with them rather than to them or at them. Remember, the best advertisements do not demand that we purchase products or use services; they illustrate the benefits we will enjoy when we choose them. The ads never sound desperate or domineering, and our favorites usually contain elements of humor. Let's learn from television advertisers and duplicate their successes. Our audiences await us.

Chapter Nine

PARENTS AND TEENS: THAT'S WHAT FRIENDS ARE FOR

Adolescence will be easier for everyone who can keep in mind that one of the fundamental tasks of the teen years is to try on new ideas and new identities. So, while our kids are entertaining different philosophies, we can either be the approachable parents to whom they will come to discuss the new ideas to which they have been exposed, or authorities who hear no opinions other than our own. Of course, the latter means we will be left out as they go to others to guide them. I believe that most of us want to be the parents who get to participate in our children's journeys.

The teen years are a sort of "home stretch"--and it is a long home stretch. These are not months, but years of intense personal examination and exploration of every aspect of the world about them, of emotional highs and lows, of changing identities and experimentation--a major, lengthy process. I am a strong believer that kids who enter this life stage having had supportive parents and abundant, hands-on experience in gradually being responsible for themselves and their decisions, possess greater self-regard. They have also acquired skills which bolster their confidence, help them succeed at their adolescent tasks, and reduce their at-risk status for premature sexual relationships, pregnancy, drug abuse, and other serious, yet common, teen problems.

Building Healthy Relationships

For most teenagers, the support network expands as their friends become a major focus in their lives, and we parents <u>seem</u> to play a minor, supporting role. Actually we are part of an essential infrastructure, not very noticeable but vital. We are always there. And although we, too, are changing and growing as we continue in our own <u>process</u>, there is a reliability to us which makes us the safe harbor, the beacon, which our children can use as a reference point.

Our sort of behind-the-scenes role does not mean that we need to stay out of the way unless beckoned. It is more about the importance of continuing our role as models of satisfying adulthood and friendship rather than as drill sergeants. In fulfillment of this role, we need to be mindful of teenagers', be they thirteen or nineteen, lasting need for our affection. This warm element of human bonding will not suddenly disappear unless it is gradually removed from your communication repertoire.

Affection with teens can be expressed in many ways: a squeeze on the arm, a knowing wink or glance, a special handshake, hugs, kisses, cuddles. Each relationship is different, and the circumstances under which we display affection vary. Especially with teens, hugging and "horseplay" are common gestures at home, but many kids prefer a more distanced and formal approach when they are in public. In healthy families, kids can express that preference without fear of hurt feelings or parental anger.

I observe that sometimes affection and interaction with kids are sorts of necessary tasks with parents, shoulds: "I really should hug my daughter/son more often," "We really ought to spend more time having fun with our kids because it's good for the family," or "I know I should visit with my daughter/son, but there never seems to be an opportunity." It becomes a task when it is no longer a natural, day-to-day part of life, the way it was when kids were young and seemed to need us more. Both generations get distracted by jobs, hobbies, television, and outside interests so that we get out of the habit of hugging, sitting and talking, just being with and for each other.

If you have lost that casual mood of closeness with your kids, it may be difficult to resurrect, but you can do it...gradually. Just as a couple must make a concerted effort to rediscover love and closeness in a marriage when they have taken each other for granted and concentrated on other things, you can take steps to reattract your teen to you.

There are unlimited ways to maintain or rebuild close relationships, and it does not take expensive and involved outings to reconnect with your child. This bond can be rebuilt as you gradually and regularly participate in some task(s) as a helper or colleague (not an expert). Perhaps you might take walks together, or visit and solicit opinions in the car to and from school. Some parents and teens take advantage of their shared interests such as sewing, auto mechanics, weight-lifting, or tennis. I know of a father who remained an active part of his daughter's adolescence through their shared interest in horses. As they cleaned stalls, repaired equipment and rode, they secured a special bond that has endured many years and miles of separation.

Our friendships start growing again when we clear the distractions, such as radio and television, and start to share our thoughts and feelings and give our children a comfortable and accepting atmosphere in which to reveal theirs. If you and your adolescent still have this special link, then you are both very fortunate. If this link has fallen into a state of disrepair, look for opportunities when you and your teen can reignite. This active choice can reap great rewards. I believe that you will start to see that your teen discovers you as a friend she wants to see more often.

Please keep in mind that just as all quality friendships develop slowly ("Beware instant intimacy," cautions Scott Peck, M.D., author of The Road Less Traveled), so, too, will this one. Connecting with your child involves a process of becoming pals. It won't happen after one big week-end or shared activity, as we have come to expect after years of watching it happen within two hours in a movie. Friendship grows gradually, each one unfolding in its own time and way.

A trusting relationship isn't just a neat thing to have with your child, should it work out that way; it is a critical element in your son's or daughter's support network during a turbulent life-stage. How many of us have heard kids say, "I didn't want him to buy me more stuff; I just wanted him to spend some time with me and show an interest in what I was doing."

We can muster the energy and resources to hustle a prospective client or customer because we are motivated to do so; we see rewards in such relationships. Attracting our teenagers is similar. If a warm connection does not exist now between you and your teen, it cannot become a reality without your personal commitment to making affinity between you a priority. You must be willing to actively pursue this friendship. You must place your child as high among priorities as prospective clients and accounts, people we would never consider putting off or keeping waiting.

Peer Friendships

A side benefit of your improved relationship with your teens may be that your children and their friends choose to spend more time at your house. When an atmosphere lacking in tension and criticism while filled with genuine acceptance and respect exists, there is a comfortable setting where kids (and adults) gravitate.

Oftentimes parents with great aspirations for their children feel threatened by the influence which their kids' friends exert and prefer that the friends not come by too often. Welcome your teenagers' friends into your world just as you would welcome their piano practicing, jazz dancing, merit badge projects, rehabilitating an old car, and other new interests. Friends are an important connection in their lives at this time, and kids are quick to feel that parents are interfering when they (parents) object to their children's choices in friends. When this happens, teens will oftentimes defend their friends and feel alienated from their parents; this is part of establishing their independence, and that's normal, too.

Teenagers are very sensitive to criticism, and many of them feel that adults admonish them wherever they go: home, school, malls, church, work, cruising. Parents who truly want their home to be a comfortable refuge for their children and friends while maintaining some level of domestic order might do well to minimize the rules and emphasize the shared ownership of the home environment.

This approach entails a basic understanding that everyone is responsible. So the children's friends are expected to treat the home environment just as the parents' friends do. In our house that would mean cleaning-up after themselves, smoking only out-of-doors, and engaging in no illegal activities. It would include keeping noise and music at levels that do not disturb others (that's why we have headphones). There do not need to be any written rules, just an understanding that there are many ways we are considerate of individual and group needs.

Kids want respect, and when parents let them know that they respect their kids enough to treat them as they do their adult friends, the teens tend to live up to the expectations. Sure, parents sometimes need to remind kids that the mess in the kitchen belongs to the kids, but there is no need to create a "them versus us" situation.

Some parents, desperate to have their kids like them and be at home as much as possible, will become virtual slaves, providing unlimited food, drink, entertainment, and maid service, permitting smoking, abusive language, and videos that they find offensive, and maybe even tolerating sexual behavior of which they disapprove. They may be saying to themselves: "We just have to make sure our kids want to be at home; otherwise they'll be on the streets getting into trouble." What the kids read in this is: "My parent(s) are doormats." And they treat their parents accordingly--not because they are bad kids, but because the parents have sent out the message that they are willing to tolerate anything. Do you think such parents are respected?

Do you think their kids say: "Gee, I want to be just like my mom/dad when I grow up?"

Teens are not fooled by this. Most parents do not allow their own friends to be abusive. Tolerating chaos does not create an environment of mutual respect and visible caring. It tells kids that the adults have resigned themselves to disorderly conduct by adolescents and do not believe that teens can be expected to do any better.

Go ahead and set limits with your children. Healthy people establish boundaries in all of their relationships, communicating which behaviors are okay and which are not. To fail to communicate our boundaries with our children is, again, to deny them the experience of real-life, healthy relationships, and such failures are red flags that we have some very serious issues of our own.

If you do not like cigarette smoke in your house, say so. Parents cannot stop kids from smoking, but they can say: "If you choose to smoke, you'll need to do so outside." Some may use and/or carry drugs. Again, a parent with good boundaries will say to a kid with drugs, "We don't permit drugs in our house; if you choose to carry them with you, then I'll know that you've also chosen not to remain here."

What I have learned to do is to articulate my position and let them make choices around that information. All the while, it is clear that I have limits. This demonstrates my self-respect and my respect for them as well. This is part of being honest with adolescents about facts, feelings, and choices. It helps parents to avoid nasty scenes where they argue about who is "right," and it gives teens experiences making decisions while they still are exposed to our values.

Might they sometimes become angry and insist that you are unreasonable because you have placed a limit on what you will permit in your home or what you are willing to do for them? Sure. And so what? Sometimes people don't like the choices that we make, but healthy adults know that it is fine to maintain order in their personal environments. Such decisions model self-regard, self-care, and good decision-making.

How can all of this possibly be about sexuality education? The ways in which we interact with other people (specifically our teenage children as our present concern) and what we model for them about mature and happy adulthood are pivotal foundation stones of strong personal identities. How we perceive ourselves and how we then communicate those self-perceptions are basic aspects of what each person's sexuality is all about. Is our model of adult sexuality a healthful and inviting one? Are we the balanced, mature individuals from whom older children seek friendship and enlightenment? Once kids reach adolescence, their information sources multiply as never before, and they will decide whom they will adopt as guides. If we want to reach them and have any impact during these years when they are pondering the really heavy issues of human sexuality we must do so at a level of friendship and mentoring, demonstrating that happy, well-adjusted adults know how to create balance and order in their own lives.

Talking About Sex

Because teens are so involved with fresh ideas and are forming and changing opinions on a monthly basis, they like being included in conversations where their opinions are actually taken seriously. Now add to that a keen interest in sexual matters, and we have the perfect formula for lots of lively discussions. Kids <u>want</u> to talk about sex!

For instance, you may discover that your child has purchased a <u>Playboy</u>/<u>Playgirl</u> magazine. This is an ordinary indicator of sexual curiosity. Please, if you are shocked, don't reveal that to your teen. At a feeling level, (s)he will probably experience shame or embarrassment if you display alarm or if you tease. Rather, accept this signal of curiosity as one of your invitations to calmly discuss values and behaviors. If you can understand that it is absolutely normal to want to look at unclothed bodies, it will help you.

Such an incident can be an opportunity or a disaster, depending upon <u>your</u> response. If you ignore it, your child has missed a chance to learn more about both sexual facts and sexual values. If you freak out, the idea is reinforced that sex is bad and dirty (and so is your child). If you initiate an ongoing dialogue open to mutual sharing, you enhance his/her understanding of life and sex's meaning in life.

And, yes, it's fine to tell your teen that just as cigarettes and drugs are not permitted in the house, nor are magazines that violate your values, if that's the case. You may choose to articulate why, but don't plead for understanding; just state your position.

Try to express your thoughts using words which are not value-laden, such as "filth," "disgusting," and "pornography." Although such words might be exact descriptions of your thoughts, your child will probably personalize those words and experience negative feelings about him/herself. Such shaming will not cause him to be more receptive to your opinions; it will only teach him to be secretive and resentful towards you.

If you have succeeded in keeping sex at a level where it is comfortably discussed, your child may explain to you why (s)he thinks such materials have some value. That does not mean that you have to agree or compromise the limits you have set, but it will be another indicator that you have established an open atmosphere.

Another area of keen curiosity is parents' sex lives. Surely you remember wondering about your folks! I know parents whose children have asked questions such as: "Do you and Mom have sex in the shower?" While we are eager to be honest and comfortable with our children's questions, the details of parents' private sexual sharing are just that: private. I encourage these parents to remember the value of personal boundaries and to reassert those limits with their children, saying something like: "Our sex life is private," or "I don't believe that's any of your business." Again, no upset, no anger, just state the facts.

In open family systems, children will bring home stories, jokes, ideas, and information from their friends. Some of what they tell you may surprise and even offend. Again, I urge you to be honest and direct. If you think the joke your fourteen-year-old just told is funny, go ahead and laugh. And if you think that it's raunchy or offensive, respond accordingly. Say so, and tell him/her why if you like.

More parents are mentioning exchanges between their children and peers which the parents believe are inappropriate. Some have spoken of junior high kids telling about boys giving girls g-strings and sexy underwear at birthday parties. One mom told of a thirteen-year-old girl asking her son if he had "gotten his red wings yet" (i.e., had sex with a menstruating girl). In light of the fact that our kids are exposed to so much "adult" humor and situations where the adults appear to be approving by their laughter, it's not terribly surprising that they try to recreate those comic situations when they get together.

If your teens are telling you similar stories, pat yourselves on the back. This sort of sharing is proof that incredibly open communication and trust exist between you. I view these moments as further proof that the kids want to talk about sex with someone they trust, respect, and with whom they feel safe. Sometimes they are seeking more factual information (Do couples have sex during menstrual periods?). At other times, they want to get some feedback about your thoughts, feelings, and values (Do you think it's funny that Jason gave Jennifer a g-string?). They want help putting these events in some sort of understandable framework for social meaning. Staying calm and rational is the key here so that these occasions are repeated.

Giving Meaning to Our Sexuality

Teens want to discuss everything: pornography, abortion, homosexual feelings, homosexual behavior, heterosexual feelings and behavior, family planning, romance, masturbation, oral sex, everything! They are figuring out more all of the time, yet they feel both vulnerable and desirous of much more information, especially our values and opinions.

There are lots of teenagers who can answer every question correctly on a test about sexual development and family planning. Yet they are still among those who become teen fathers and mothers and who contract and transmit STDs each year. Facts are not enough when learning how to live life, including this part of life. Even well-informed adolescents are hungry for more in-depth understanding about how sex is related to feelings, what makes relationships lasting and enriching or dysfunctional, "true love," responsible behavior in varying situations, etc. Those things do not appear in too many sex education textbooks. Even if they did, words on pages would never be enough.

Rather, they come from life and living and from understanding adults who can share some of their insights about life with honesty. Adolescents need people who will say: "When I first had sex, I really didn't intend for it to happen, but...," or "Let me tell you about a big mistake I made when I was sixteen," or "I used to believe otherwise, but my experiences and observations have caused me to change my mind about_____," or "I'm so glad I made the decision to _____. This is how I think my life is different because of that choice..." These are acknowledgements that there are <u>emotional</u> and <u>experiential</u> as well as informational components to quality sexuality education.

So talk to your child and <u>with</u> your child. Continue the work that you started earlier, of using television programs, news stories, and personal experiences as starting points to address issues like teen pregnancy, sexually transmitted diseases, sexual harassment, the lines guys use on girls, and girls on guys, to pressure each other for sex. Discuss <u>how</u> abstinence from sexual intercourse is a positive life choice at this time in their lives. Discuss sexual arousal and some of the creative and risk-free ways of meeting this normal human response while developing an exciting understanding of sexual pleasuring. Talk about family planning, not just in terms of how each method works but also the considerations people might entertain when selecting a form. Discuss this as it relates to STDs (sexually transmitted diseases).

If you think that you do not know enough about these subjects, call your city or county health department or a community organization for some of their brochures, or arrange for one of their staff to come to your church/temple/neighborhood organization for an informative presentation. These professionals are eager to get the word out among caring people in the community who will use that knowledge to positively affect others. If you cannot arrange for a speaker, ask them to send you some of their brochures. Use your public librarians' resource skills. Read your daily newspaper and weekly news magazines; they regularly report about sexual health issues. It's okay to look up from the morning newspaper and say: "Gee, listen to this..." Then read the main points in an article about STDs, homosexual marriages, etc. Or turn down the TV volume during a commercial so that you can react to a morning news program's story.

"But isn't family planning information just permission to 'do it'?"

Some parents do not want their children to know anything about family planning, fearing that with this information and access to contraceptives, their children will start having sexual intercourse. I disagree. I think that a much better route is to offer children an all-inclusive education about human sexuality within the framework of our values and an understanding of the societal messages which subtly and overtly encourage casual sexual behavior.

Hiding information and treating teens as if they cannot possibly master their biological urges is demeaning. Denying them information which might prevent a pregnancy or the transmission of an STD, should they become sexually active anyway, could be lethal.

I have seen too much of teen pregnancy, abortion, parenting, and sexually transmitted diseases. While I hope for teens to make the active choice to knowledgeably postpone sexual intercourse, I realize that once they decide to engage in sex and are committed to that course, it is far better to do everything possible to prevent conception and infection.

Abigail Van Buren (Dear Abby) recently printed some figures gathered by the Alan Guttmacher Institute regarding the suprise pregnancy rates of family planning methods. Beside each method was its effectiveness **In Theory** and then **In Reality**. That column said so much in a small space about the unintended pregnancy risks couples assume--even when they are "being careful." Tap into this resource. Use it! Rather than saying, "Neal, be sure you take a look at **Dear Abby** today," try an approach which treats him as a bright equal, not a pupil: "Gee, did you see these surprise pregnancy rates that **Dear Abby** printed today? I had no idea that so many people still get pregnant even when they are taking precautions." Say it with a voice that encourages comments.

Teens view Ms. Van Buren and her sister, Ann Landers, as friends and resources, helpers to us all through the tough times. Their columns present perfect openers for discussions about sexual issues. So I suggest that you use available pieces such as this one to talk about subjects which not only interest your kids but about which they are getting exposure elsewhere.

Date Rape

Make sure that you do not ignore the subject of date rape. No parent wants his/her son accused of rape during a date because he never got the message that no matter how aroused he may be (and she may <u>seem</u> to be), he must <u>never</u> force a girl/woman to have sexual relations. If she says "no," every guy needs to know to treat that word like a loaded gun, and do as the lady says: stop.

Daughters should become acquainted with situations and behaviors which are likely to present confusion or provocation. The messages of body language and verbal declarations are not always harmonious.

Teach your daughters to express what they mean, <u>clearly</u>. Mixed messages, in any forum, hinder precise communication. This means allowing and encouraging our daughters to be direct in <u>all</u> of their social interactions-- including their interactions with us at home. Precise communication is a learned skill which each of us needs if we are to be effective in work and personal situations. Girls who are comfortable expressing their opinions and needs without concern for others' approval are much more capable of keeping themselves safe in dating situations.

This brings us back to the awareness that learning to make wise sexual decisions is not a task separate from the rest of our other life choices. If I lack confidence and need others' approval in general social situations, if I am indirect in expressing my preferences and needs during the regular course of business, I will not have the necessary tools to be comfortable with <u>my</u> desire to refrain from sexual advances nor to express that desire succinctly.

Sorting Out the Messages

Today's teens live during a time of tremendous sexual chaos. Previous generations were not raised in such sexually saturated cultures plagued by STDs, fragmented families, and the constant media portrayal and general acceptance of casual sex and violence against women. To be in the midst of this with little or no rational direction from adults who have sorted it out is unconscionable. Talk to your children! Help them create some order of society's mixed messages.

When you have watched a movie or heard a story and, again, the partners have jumped into bed the moment they get a little horny or think they might be in love, <u>talk about it:</u>.

- How did it happen?
- What lines did they use?
- How did each of them communicate willingness: verbally, with their bodies, clothing, the location they chose at the end of their evening out (a drink at his place rather than a drink at a local piano bar)?
- Is that the best or only way to communicate physical attraction and love?
- What other things might they have done?
- In what ways did the characters' sexual involvement affect their relationship and/or other aspects of their lives? Give examples.
- What other love-enhancing behaviors did the characters develop as we watched their relationship progress?
- What things did you see in the relationship that make you think they are capable of a

long-term, happy romance? Give specific examples.

- Why do you think they chose sexual intercourse so soon after meeting each other?
- What do responsible people do when they're feeling really hot?
- Talk about risky sexual practices (no condoms, multiple partners, etc.) and analyze the scene in relation to what we know about optimizing health.
- If the characters were married to others, ask your kids how they think they would feel if their spouses had sex with someone else. Or how would they feel if one of their parents had another relationship which was sexual?
- Get into the feelings that the characters exhibit. Acknowledge how attractive the portrayal seems, and help your kids bring it back into reality.

The possibilities are endless provided you make this a discussion, not a lecture. There are a lot of themes in the list above. Don't try to cover every concept each time you talk about sex and relationships. Just toss some of these considerations (or others which are important to you) into conversations anytime it seems comfortable. The goal is to help our children develop their analytical abilities so that they can evaluate the messages all around them in order to consciously make wise personal choices.

As you can see, these themes are about what sexual acts communicate and how they affect people and their relationships. The focus is on the meanings we attach to our acts and how these influence our choices, personal growth and satisfaction, and how they impact our responsibilities to the larger human family. So it's okay to let them know about your beliefs. If you can calmly articulate <u>why</u> you respond as you do and how you believe TV and movie sex impact viewers' daily lives, you'll get a lively discussion going <u>only</u> if your voice and body language make it very clear that everybody's opinions are welcome. No one in the discussion is "the authority." This is not a debate contest where somebody has to win. It is a chance for your kids to hear a new slant on the subject of sexual expression and for you to learn where they are emotionally and philosophically.

All of these occasions are great times to do more than critique sexual and romantic interactions between individuals. They are ideal occasions to talk about and highlight <u>healthy</u> romance. Some teens have never actually heard someone they know in a quality adult relationship admit that being aroused is warm and pleasurable. Teens' exposure is mostly limited to sexual arousal as an intense and irresistable experience among movie characters who are out of control and whose relationships lack trust and commitment. This portrayal (usually by adults) models the very worst for teens and helps explain the romantic myths that they hang onto about sex:

- Sex should just happen.
- Planned sex is boring.
- Fighting and angry tension add zest and even stability to relationships.
- Nice girls don't even anticipate sexual intercourse; they get carried away by the passion of the experience (and therefore nice girls don't contracept).

- There is no such thing as a couple that sits down during a time when neither is aroused, mutually agrees on a limit for their sexual intimacy, and sticks to the limit.

For their sake, we must be willing to take teens beyond the myths and bring them to an "Age of Enlightenment." To do this, we will need to recognize that teens not only fantasize about being in love and sexual intimacy, they become intensely aroused and want to be able to talk about appropriate and responsible ways of addressing their feelings, desires, and urges. They want excitement and thrills and to be "in love." So far, they have been shown only limited avenues for obtaining these experiences. And the ones which society presents to them are filled with hazards (i.e., impulsive sexual intercourse and multiple partners).

How about filling in the gaps and exposing them to a more generous repertoire that has the richness of hugging, massage, hand holding, smiles and whispers, caressing, and creative kissing, sharing inner thoughts, participating in mutually enjoyable activities?

Think about the movies again. The passionate sex scenes are powerful because we have watched the characters briefly bond with each other through very ordinary, non-genital activities: walking in Central Park or along a California beach, struggling with a problem or emergency situation, or maybe sharing a cause or concern. Lovers, and others who aspire to be lovers, need more examples of how to build bonds which are real and can sustain the test of time, to create a firm foundation in a relationship so that, when they come together sexually, a relationship exists which is worthy of such a powerful expression.

Balance society's unrealistic messages with openness and a willingness to talk about sexual thoughts and feelings as being okay. Recognize fantasies as an important part of sexual development and continuing pleasure. Remember that teens need to see romance alive and well in our own relationships and honesty about the ups and downs of love and life. This does not mean that we tell our children intimate details that are private, but we can talk about challenges that we have faced, individually and as couples, and how we have dealt with them. It doesn't hurt teens to know that their parents were growing apart at one point and then made a conscious effort to get their marriage back on track, that rather than resort to extra-marital affairs, they refocused their energy on their relationship. Adolescents need to know that adults have wishes and desires and that they, too, make responsible choices that are consistent with long-term goals.

Help them see how sexual actions can have major consequences which we oftentimes do not consider. The stories and statistics on news programs are very available references filled with real-life, personal stories of people whose hopes and dreams are just like ours, but who will never be the same because of the sexual risks they took. Kids need help distinguishing between the fantasy love and sexual models of TV and film and the real world, where people bond with each other during sexual intercourse, where people attach expectations to relationships that have become sexual, where babies are conceived, etc.

Compare sexual behavior and decision-making to other areas of life. A universally recognized measure of maturity is the ability to pause and consider the pros and cons prior to making an important decision and taking action.

Immature individuals are more impulsive and act without careful thought. People who take good care of themselves and who are cautious not to hurt or exploit others deliberate before engaging in sexual intimacy with others. Help them see that, in the real world, to engage in sexual intercourse is a <u>major life choice</u> and, therefore, should be made following careful deliberation, not simply in response to arousal.

Talk about how our sexual choices fit in with our immediate and long term goals. What do these choices mean for me (a teen) today and in the years to come?

- Consider how the choice to move to a more advanced stage of sexual intimacy is also a conscious choice to step that much closer to sexual intercourse.
- How is love best expressed at various life stages and love relationship stages?
- What do they want to express through sexual intimacy? Do their choices express that?
- If it is love they think they are communicating, is it loving to engage in an activity that will result in the next two weeks of the girlfriend worrying whether or not she's going to get her period? For a boy to be placed at risk for eighteen years of child support payments which he is presently unprepared to assume?
- If a baby is out of the question at this stage in their lives (finishing high school or college), is behavior which might create a baby a good choice right now?
- What do they think men/women want in their love relationships? Why? Is this different from what teens want?

- In what ways is masturbation a positive or negative sexual choice in terms of personal goals and desires?
- Discuss the incremental steps from exchanging interested glances to hand-holding, to hugging, kissing, caressing above and below the waist, petting to orgasm, oral stimulation to orgasm, and sexual intercourse.

There needs to be an awareness that their sexual decision-making does not occur in a vacuum, although it may seem that way in the midst of passion. Discussing these ideas within the context of real events and experiences makes them believable and more interesting.

Our own stories and those of others who they know or have observed in articles, books, movies, and news stories help our children to have a much better handle on the role of human sexuality in life. Anecdotes bring the abstract to life, especially when we get a real grasp for the issues, feelings, thoughts, and motivations with which the characters struggle. Consider the example literature has served to enlighten us through stories about other people's experiences, personalizing the lessons authors wish to reveal. Stories have been used throughout human history to edify and challenge. Lessons, placed in the context of life events, are more easily understood and remembered.

These discussions are opportunities to dispel the myths about sex and love while our teens (and their parents) broaden their vision. So talk with your kids whenever there's a comfortable opportunity, and be attentive to signs that they want to talk, too. They desire and need reflections, understanding, and respect--especially from you.

Going for the Gold

I view the dating years as a lengthy period of training, just like aspiring athletes require when they strive to become Olympic-calibre competitors. Athletes do not become world-class because they have simple fantasies of winning international meets, enjoy watching exciting sporting events, or because they put on the right gear. They train and refine their skills. They learn to become the masters of their bodies, to be disciplined rather than impulsively responding to every urge. It is a <u>process</u>, one which makes significant demands and, therefore, brings tremendous personal satisfaction.

Isn't it time to tell our kids the truth about love and romance,that they need to train if they want to be truly adept, and if they want world-class emotional and physical satisfaction? Why do we hang onto this idea that all it takes to be a good lover is good looks, a hot body, an intriguing location, and someone to whom we are attracted at the moment?

Few of us instinctively possess the interpersonal skills which build <u>real</u> intimacy. Unfortunately, our preoccupation with sex is distracting us from developing those skills, the foundation for Olympic-calibre love lives. We must allow ourselves the time to learn the art of blending our emotional and intellectual commitments with our sexual involvement so that the two are balanced, just as a skater works with her music, timing, gravity, and momentum. Her routine is only an act of beauty when there is balance and harmony, proof of her commitment to the daily challenges.

Isn't it important to model and talk about these so that your child has a better understanding of the power of sexual feelings and behaviors? Why not guide him/her to take time and care before crossing the line to the next level of physical involvement? Isn't she entitled to information which will assist her as she trains so that she understands how her choices are related to her goal attainment? Coaches give their pupils guidance for greatness, not merely caution to avoid pitfalls.

Your discussions can help your child establish a sexual agenda, making sexuality a recognized and honored part of being a human being, identifying a meaningful place for it in their lives, and removing that pathetic excuse: "Well, it just happened."

And What If They Just Don't Buy It?

Sometimes you may feel disturbed when your children seem to be drifting from your values, and you may want to rein them in, putting some distance between them and those who influence them with different views. That is insulting to bright children, and they will view you as a tyrant and your opinions as suspect. People who possess values which they cherish, and who understand why they believe as they do, are not filled with fear that their views will be rejected; nor do they fear those who hold differing points of view. Rather, they see that they have something worthwhile and enlightening, and others are attracted to them and their articulation of those values.

What I am saying is that if you are hopeful that your children will adopt your values, I urge you to live those values cheerfully and to speak of them openly with your children. But if you attempt to force them upon your children, I think that you will be in for many heated arguments and a great deal of resistance and rejection.

By this time, what we can do best is to LISTEN, EMPATHIZE, SHARE, ACCEPT, and MODEL. That doesn't mean that we must always agree. But when we accept our kids where they are and give them room to consider new ideas, while still being loving with each other, we have a much better chance of raising children who can examine issues without feeling threatened and developing belief systems that are really theirs.

Oftentimes, too, kids stray for awhile, adopt opinions we reject or make some decisions which cause them (and usually us, too) heartache and difficulties. Only later do they learn to create order. If they have been raised in houses where failures are catastrophes and causes for shame, then their abilities to recover from their mistakes will be delayed and limited. If they are fortunate enough to come from homes where mistakes are viewed as part of the roller coaster ride of life (lots of ups and downs; it's all part of the process), then they will be better equipped to bounce back. The infrastructure will be there--in their parents and within themselves.

And some of our children will adopt value systems different from ours, never to believe as we do. Those who maintain that only people who agree with them are good people will shut their children out of their lives or express their resentments for noncompliance in petty ways. Those who believe that there is enough room on this planet for diverse opinions, and that there are good people who do not agree with us, will continue to welcome their children and enjoy lasting friendships.

There is no best way, no single way of giving your child a full understanding of what it means to be a healthy sexual being. Each person's sexual socialization begins when (s)he first emerges from the womb and continues as long as (s)he lives. The more you know and love yourself, the healthier your relationships and the better your chances of passing on a strong sense of the meaning of being a man, a woman, and in relationship with others. This lifelong process is a bit like a recipe that needs constant attention. We add various ingredients along the way, sometimes the same ones several times, patiently tending to our invention and enjoying the creative process itself.

Starting early is best, but because we humans are so resilient and flexible, we can always begin right where we are today. For as one Dallas minister says when asked for the time, the answer is "now." Now. It is what we have with the past behind us and the future in many ways uncertain.

So with your child, now, communicate love, interest, understanding and acceptance, and the information (s)he deserves. Communicate your hopes, knowledge and feelings, your lack of knowledge, and a willingness to find the answers together. With those honest qualities present in your relationship, you will be the teacher, mentor, and friend that every child deserves.

And finally, once you have done your best with the now, the present moment that you have with your children, let go. Remember that we cannot control our children's feelings and behaviors; nor can we undo our mistakes or theirs. And they will make mistakes; they must make mistakes in order to be actively about the journey of life.

Every parent will wish that (s)he had done some things a little differently. That's life. I have never met a perfect parent, and I know that I never will. So I encourage you to lighten up on yourself, celebrate what you do well, and get on with what you have... now.

Chapter Ten

EXPOSING THE CASUAL SEX MYTH

If one of your children had a new car, carefully purchased with money saved from jobs, holiday and birthday gifts, and maybe even with some of your help, one might suppose that a knowledgeable and interested parent might be eager to impart some information about how to care for the new vehicle so that it would serve the owner well. We might mention something about the importance of adhering to the manufacturer's maintenance schedule (especially while the car is under warranty), keeping the tires properly inflated and rotated, and protecting the paint with a high quality wax. We would make sure that the subject of drinking and driving had been a frequent topic because of social responsibility, our concern for our child's and friends' well-being, and the car. No doubt we would reach an agreement on responsibility for insurance, and we would discuss which friends ought to be trusted in the driver's seat.

The underlying messages would be that human safety is of primary importance, and this car is expensive, so treat it with care. As we would have been car owners for years, our children would have observed our own on-going maintenance efforts, so there would be a consistent message in our actions to reinforce our words.

Imagine that, over the years when your child was getting interested in vehicles, car commercials and automotive-oriented shows on the television and in movies somehow managed to consistently demonstrate a careless attitude towards driving and car maintenance. Maybe in movies they would regularly show people leaving the lights on for hours and then the ignition still working when the characters returned to their cars. What if you saw weekly portrayals of people drinking and then driving with total control and quick reflexes? How do you think you might react if, while watching TV and movies with your kids, you saw programming that showed teens driving recklessly while never having collisions? Would it be believable to you if the character's car was in perfect condition, shiny and dentless, even though in previous weeks we had seen the car rolled, kicked, left in the desert for days, and always parked in the sun?

Do you suppose that if you viewed such portrayals that no one in your house would say something like: "Oh, that's so phoney!" I can hear the remarks now: "Did you see that?!!!," " "Oh, come on, it doesn't turn out that way...," or "I sure wish they'd make cars like that for the rest of us!" We would be impatient with and critical of such faulty presentations. If car care were our personal interest and we hoped that our child would share in our hobby, we would undoubtedly point out the inconsistencies to him/her.

American children are exposed to the commercial messages of television and movies as no other generation or culture before. What do those media convey about caring for one's fertility? About romance and lasting commitments? About love? How do we adults respond to these unrealistic scenes?

Children's sexuality models, as portrayed by the media, foster the notion that the best language of love is sexual intercourse, and that such a choice rarely has unwelcome consequences. Those models reveal a passionate, steamy urgency to which any half-awake sexual being can immediately relate, but they consistently fail to give the bigger picture. They sell us on the thrill with little or no reference to the concerns that follow after the lights are turned on, and the partners get dressed. Rarely do they attempt to approximate the lasting emotional and physical pain that millions of Americans experience annually because of poor sexual choices: STDs, surprise pregnancies, abortions, infertility, infecting unsuspecting partners, emotional upsets, etc.

The insidious message is that sex is neat, fun, and a carefree pastime. The reality is that premature sexual involvement is fraught with alarming hazards.

So why are we so silent about the most visible sexual models of this culture, which lure kids (and adults) into believing that casual sex and numerous partners have few consequences? Why do we continue pretending that our emotions, fertility, and relationship skills are unaffected when we adopt an almost indifferent attitude about human sexual behavior? I can think of no other behavior that gets this special treatment: engaging in the behavior is isolated from the rest of one's life and functioning.

Our children are in the daily audiences for whom these seemingly real portrayals are made. But, unfortunately, when they go out and follow the examples which they have been watching for years, things rarely work out so smoothly. For them, premature sexual involvement is fraught with alarming consequences for which commercial breaks offer no relief. Yet, as a nation we have thrown in the towel and have become not only tolerant but accepting of society's prototypes of adult romantic relationships and of the resulting early onset of teen sex.

I have heard lots of adults say that there is no point trying to discourage teens from premature sexual involvements, because it just can't be done. How often I have heard: "Be realistic. They're going to do it anyway, so we should just make sure they have protection." I hear several things in that all-too-common response, and little of what I am hearing is helping kids.

• First of all, the resignation that this attitude expresses is a handy excuse for doing nothing. At best, we endorse careful contraceptive use, even though we know that teens are notoriously poor users of family planning methods. Talk about "magical thinking"!

So we just leave our kids hanging out there with only this sex-is-best example to follow. I wonder if our own constant exposure to TV and movies has rendered us complacent, if we, too, believe that casual sex is the norm and that, somehow, people today have less ability to master their sexual urges than past generations. Is this the best that we have to offer our children?

• Our silence is a testimonial to our own unwillingness to deal with the danger that sexual experimentation poses for our kids. When we read about the consequences of adolescent sexual behavior in the paper or watch news programs, the statistics are about people "out there"--not our children, not people we know. But our kids are part of the population that is high-risk for high-stakes problems. As if pregnancy were not reason enough to discourage teens from intercourse while encouraging other attitudes and behaviors, we are looking at a growing body of sexually transmitted diseases (STDs) which are antibiotic-resistant. New infections of the A.I.D.S. virus are declining in the gay population and rising in teen and female populations. Girls who have multiple partners (and they will if they begin having sex as teens) have a much greater incidence of pelvic inflammatory disease (PID), a leading cause of female sterility. Connections are also being made between infections from sexual practices and cervical cancer. I know of a wealthy Texas family whose young, college-graduate daughter recently learned that she is HIV-positive. By most standards today, she would not be considered promiscuous, and she is absolutely heterosexual; yet she is paying dearly for having been taken in with the dominant cultural message that sex is no big deal.

So why are we sitting here in silence when our kids are exposed to <u>years</u> of casual sexual portrayals without realistic consequences? Would we be tight-lipped if the programming made drug use look equally carefree?

• When we express resignation to teen sex because "no one can stop them" and "they're going to do it anyway," don't we communicate a sorry lack of respect for our children? Aren't we in fact saying to them: "You are so weak and foolish, so very incapable, that you cannot intelligently respond to your sexual drives. In fact, you lack sufficient brain power, common sense, and motivation to do anything except copulate." Aren't we also saying to them that there is no alternative to sexual intercourse for their romantic and sexual expressions?

We want our kids to develop some degree of personal discipline regarding alcohol use, television viewing, food intake, expression of anger, and money management. But we are implicitly designating sexual conduct as an area beyond them for mastery. Why do we underestimate our capable children, and why do we actually deny them opportunities to expand their repertoire for romantic expressions?

The Price Tag Includes More Than Pregnancy and Diseases.

Teenagers are not younger versions of adults, even though their bodies make them appear so. Emotionally and developmentally, they are in a considerable state of transition, and this is a critical area for our focus.

Intimate sexual involvement requires a well-integrated self if it is to be a <u>long-term</u>, enriching experience. You see, we bond with our partners during this intense physical, emotional, even spiritual event. When a teen, who is still in the process of completing a large share of his/her identity formation engages in this activity which demands so much of the self, that kid's personal program is grossly accelerated. (S)he is taking on adult involvements before (s)he has completed the essential infrastructure for who (s)he is.

Admittedly, there are a lot of pressures and tremendous instability in teen's lives. Getting the feeling of belonging to someone through an exclusive relationship, which is heightened by the sexual component, provides young people with a temporary sanctuary and a surreal sense of identity and attachment. But rarely, very rarely, does the relationship have the foundation to support this exaggerated <u>feeling</u> of love and affinity. This feeling is almost like the sensation that a new homeowner has about a palatial new residence, not realizing that it is built on a not-yet-settled landfill; the house is too much for the shaky foundation. What happens when the house begins to crack?

Because teens are in such an important and fast-paced growth process, it is natural for them to move in and out of romantic relationships. Emotional trouble enters the picture when the intense relationship, which includes sex and its powerful bonding properties, ends. An adolescent psyche, not yet fully matured, is taxed beyond a reasonable level, and such a sophisticated involvement can be more than a fragile identity can handle. Now, imagine what multiple superbondings (through sexual intercourse) followed by subsequent uncouplings do for a young man or woman who is still in the process of serious identity formation. Not a pleasant thought.

I have worked with teens near suicide over broken relationships. In each case, I believe that they have over-invested their incomplete emotional structures through sexual bonding, and they are not yet equipped with a solid sense of self nor the coping skills to deal with the pain of separation and rejection.

Why do we perpetuate this myth that intercourse is the best language of love? Why are we unwilling to expose this model as a sham? Are we honestly unaware of the adverse affects that sexual bonding has on our children's emotional development? Don't we know that real and lasting intimacy is created out of friendship, sharing, trust and security, ingredients which require attention, time, effort, and increasing wisdom? How can we possibly believe that our cultural focus on sex is assisting our children in their skill building for first-class love? Isn't it time to offer adolescents some new models for love and romance?

We are so cautious with our small children, making sure that they are adequately protected from even minor threats and making sure that they are not exposed to ideas and activities before they are developmentally ready. Knowing what we do about the adverse results of premature sexual experiences for teens, we must provide some protection for them as well. We must stop the abandonment of our teenagers and create a new model which can work in their lives and which <u>they</u> will want to incorporate into their dating behavior.

Rewriting our script

We no longer have the societal framework in place to maintain sexual intercourse as a privilege for adults in committed relationships. And we should not count on suddenly seeing a decline in fantasy television and movie sex scenes. If we are committed to acknowledging the cultural influences and providing new ideas and opportunities about love and romance for kids, we must accept that <u>we</u> will be prominent players in helping our kids to understand the messages about them and in modeling more appropriate responses to the wondrous feelings of love and arousal.

First, we must move beyond the old hazard-focused approach to teen sex which rarely works anymore. That method usually involves warning kids about all of the awful things that can happen to them should they engage in genital sexual behaviors. Rarely does such advice occur in the context of healthful and attractive alternatives and a life history of family comfort with sexuality. More than anything else, those negative warnings have underpinnings of an anti-sex mentality. The hazard approach only addresses the troubles people encounter from poor sexual choices. This makes sense to adults because it reflects adult thinking: avoid hazards so you will live a long time. Kids, however, are not worried about life ending, and they engage in a fair degree of "magical thinking" which means, "it will never happen to me." They do not relate to the cautious approach.

We must redesign our approach and follow the example of the very commercial media who have lured kids into believing that casual sex is consequence-free. Those brilliant writers appeal to kids because they make good things happen in the lives of the actors and actresses; they portray people experiencing life seemingly to the fullest. Successful advertising is the result of careful research into human thinking and behavior. We should use their work as one of our resources.

In the late 1980s, advertisers convinced teenagers that jeans with holes were more fashionable than those without. So thousands of teens actually paid more for ripped jeans. This marketing coup was accomplished through positive associations.

I am proposing that parents not limit themselves to exposing the myths about teen sex. Yes, explore the unrealistic scenes you watch together on your favorite evening soap opera. Now, go beyond that. Look at other successful campaigns; we have turned the smoking issue around so that, now, more adolescents (especially better-educated, more upwardly mobile) view the choice to not smoke as being freeing, more life-enhancing, definitely more sophisticated. We have created the image that living a smoke-free life is really being "alive with pleasure." That's what positive associations are all about. They attract people.

We must begin promoting the decision to postpone sexual intercourse as a positive, freeing choice at this time in our children's lives. We need to elevate mastering one's sexual drives as a characteristic of winners, just like the winners who postpone certain pleasures while concentrating on others so that they can enjoy athletic, academic, and career successes, and the status and rewards which accompany those accomplishments.

This does not mean that we urge our kids to be asexual; it means that we talk about and model other, more appropriate avenues for sexual expression. It means that we help our children see that they can free themselves for other, more enduring achievements. I like the way these authors stated it:*

> Teens need reasons to believe that delaying pregnancy and parenthood is in their best interests. Our task is not merely to persuade teens to wait, but to provide...positive and rewarding options so that he/she can personally see the benefits of waiting."

This philosophy applies equally to delaying intercourse, the cause of pregnancy and parenthood.

While some adults believe it is utterly impossible for teens to forego sexual intercourse, others, frustrated by America's lack of progress in this area, are willing to entertain new possibilities. Yet, it is the teens themselves who offer me encouragement that this is a viable approach.

I have addressed and worked with so very many high school and college students who have convinced me that

---

* Adams, G., Adams-Taylor, S. & Pittman, K. (1989). Adolescent Pregnancy and Parenthood: A Review of the Problem, Solutions, and Resources. Family Relations, 38, p. 225. Reprinted with permission.

they are eager for a new model of sexual behavior and romance. They see the marriages of those ten, twenty, and thirty years older, and there are few which they would like to emulate. These students express honest concern that they are getting into the same rut that they see their elders in: relying on sex to be the primary romantic communication system in relationships. And sex isn't enough.

When I present them with the idea that they can choose to be in training to become skilled lovers for lasting relationships, I have their attention. Every one of them knows that orgasm is the max, and it is even better if you have somebody helping you to achieve it. But orgasm still isn't the foundation of a love relationship; sex alone does not have what it takes to create soulmates. They want to learn how to create and participate in relationships that will give them lifelong comfort and pleasure, real intimacy, and they know that sex is not teaching them how to get that. Some, usually the older students, even suspect that sex is getting in the way.

I never tell these students what to do. I tell them about some of my life experiences, my observations, studies conducted in the fields of human behavior and relationships, and what I think are choices which positively impact relationships. I speak as someone who has been in training, who has enjoyed and continues to experience a relationship rich in romance and caring, and who wants them to have that, too. I talk about what I see working and not working, and we explore <u>together</u> the nuances of self-expression and being in healthy, happy relationships.

The concept of <u>training</u> is one which we explore at length. We acknowledge that the greatest athletes continue training throughout their careers. The master musicians of our time practice for hours each day, including scales and chords which bear little resemblance to the dramatic performances we hear in concert halls. So, too, do great lovers continue training as they pursue their careers as committed, exciting, and evolving men and women who are capable of reaching ever greater heights of relationship fulfillment. They understand that lasting and satisfying relationships are always in the process of unfolding. A deep inner wisdom tells these young people that the goal of loving is to be intimately connected emotionally, then to renew and celebrate that love over and over again.

For one day or a few days, I can be the sounding-board and model they seek, but I cannot be the substitute for parents and a personal support network providing a daily environment in which they can explore these issues of human sexuality and, hopefully, witness romance and love.

From _you_ teens need positive modeling about love and commitment, proof that love does not die with marriage. From you they need a safe home environment in which to question and explore the issues of life. They need daily reassurances of their capabilities and goodness, appropriate affection, respect for their thoughts and feelings, and honest answers to their inquiries. Kids need parents who _understand_ their powerful sexual urges, who convey that understanding, and who help them to deal with it appropriately. They need parents who can help them distinguish between love, their search for intimacy, and their basic desire for sexual satisfaction--all good, all normal, all entitled to being differentiated and addressed. They need for _you_ to be willing to challenge the teen sex myth that says teen sex is a predetermined step. From _you_ they need a better vision of how to acquire the skills that great lovers possess.

Our family was in the Rio Grande Valley recently, and we were dinner guests of some lifetime friends of my family, a couple in their late sixties. As the husband and wife waited at the beginning of the buffet line, we noticed the wife pat the sides of her husband's waist, ever so gently, playfully, and lovingly. We visited them while they were in the midst of a family crisis, yet they still exchanged the little "I love you" gestures that make longtime marriages daily celebrations rather than endurance tests. They were real life, very available models to us and to our children about the skills of being great and happy lovers.

Such couples are around, maybe not many; but if you look, you will find them. They are among the models we need to highlight, just as we would a beautiful old car that has been carefully maintained or restored. The combination of lasting love and excitement do not happen by accident with cars...or in relationships.

In my work with students, I find that they reveal true relief when I offer them new approaches to sexual expression, something other than intercourse. There is a terrible pressure now for teens to be "sexually active" (i.e., intercourse), and many feel apologetic when they are not. At the same time, they feel ill-equipped to explain why it is not a good choice for them at this time in their lives. Some speak of their first sexual experience as something they just had to get out of the way because it was expected. Many have never entertained the notion that there are options other than intercourse, for no one has modeled alternatives or logically made a case for them. Many express an inability to direct their love expressions for better results. Some even liken their limited abilities to a sort of paralysis: they want to try some other affection expressions, but they don't know what else to do. They have been raised with a goal-oriented approach to affection and pleasuring. The goal is orgasm, and, unfortunately, the experience is short-lived.

We owe it to our teenagers to present a more realistic picture than the dominant orgasm-focused approach. I have said it so many times because it is so: I have never heard any experts report that sexual intercourse is good for teenagers. To the contrary, they see early experimentation as detrimental to development. American youth cannot afford our extravagant complacence.

I am urging you to look at this as a physical and emotional health issue for your children. We would not give in to polio if it were still a health risk today, and so we must stop resigning ourselves to risky sexual behaviors which upset the physical <u>and</u> emotional harmony of our children now and into their adulthood.

For the good of our children, we must look for occasions to model and explore lively and enriching love expressions. In the process, we will enjoy ourselves and teach our children a more expansive love language and give them permission to entertain the delight of varying levels of intimacy. Everyone's lives can be richer...including your own.

Chapter Eleven

BRIDGING THE GAP

I have told you that it is time for us to start helping our children to distinguish between fantasy and reality in media and real-life relationships. I have urged you to speak openly and frequently with your children about the advantages of postponing sexual intercourse in their love relationships. And I have encouraged you to become models of satisfying love and enriching romance in your own adult interactions. Now it is time for me to be more specific with you about what I mean when I suggest teaching our kids the concept of "more appropriate avenues for sexual expression." Without a doubt, I find this the most difficult and challenging task in our undertaking as our children's primary sexuality educators.

Most parents hope that their children's romantic relationships will be light and carefree, and that the exchanges will remain at the innocent levels of handholding and kissing, possibly some light "petting." Knowing the freedom our children might enjoy if they steer clear of premature sexual involvements, we have hung onto this age-old parental hope. However, the chance for our kids to enjoy courtships uncomplicated by too much sex too soon has become increasingly less likely, as each generation in the past forty years has been exposed to ever-greater amounts of tolerance of premature and inappropriate sexual intimacy. In the 1990s, parents' dream of no sexual experimentation remains a valid hope--but an unlikely one if parents and other sensitive and insightful sources maintain their silence about sexual feelings and behaviors. We must stop pretending that our children would never engage in intimate sexual behaviors, or that those who do are limited to the option of intercourse. This chapter is written to help you with the middle ground, to start looking at options with which we can acquaint our adolescents so that they will succeed not only in staying away from high-risk behaviors but will learn the dynamics of emotional and physical love expressions. We have to give up pretending that kids have only two sexual options: "going all the way" or nothing. We have to start talking about the area between nothing and "all the way" and helping our kids see what the possibilities are as they progress developmentally and in their love relationships.

A New Focus: From Genitals to Gentle Loving

Language reflects culture, and in this culture most of our vocabulary for sexual behavior is intercourse-focused. "Doing it," "going all the way," "making love" are just a few of the terms used to mean engaging in sexual intercourse, whether or not honest, committed love is a factor. Even the word "foreplay" is about intercourse. "Foreplay" conveys prep work, kind of like warming-up and stretching-out prior to the real workout. Foreplay is a mere preliminary for the big event, the real business of sexual intimacy.

Our kids don't want to be second-tier players, and they have picked up on the dominant notion that anything which falls short of intercourse really isn't varsity. Both our vocabulary and our focus on orgasm rather than tenderness, caring, and commitment are part of the problem. The messages are:

- that orgasm (usually via intercourse) is the highest standard of love expression--the goal; and

- that other forms of intimacy are merely steps on the way to the goal rather than being special--events in themselves.

We are communicating a very narrow concept as we continue to approach sex with our children exclusively in terms of "doing it" or "not doing it." We are overlooking the fact that there is an incredibly broad spectrum of incremental love expressions out there between sitting across the room smiling and hopping in the sack. No one else is talking to our kids about a focus other than intercourse. So tremendous pressure is placed on kids to pursue sexual behaviors even when, on their own and without societal pressure, they might concentrate on other aspects of the relationship or feel less compelled to rush things sexually.

I have discussed the importance of talking to your children about their sexual urges and loving feelings. Kids need for us to be honest with them about the many ways of responsibly expressing those urges and feelings. Just as parents can talk about how they adjusted their study skills as they moved from elementary to middle school and then to high school, now they need to talk about age, situation-appropriate, and enjoyable ways of addressing relationships and sexual urges while growing as individuals and demonstrating honest regard for boy/girlfriends.

Such on-going discussions are the times to talk about masturbation and reinforce its place in healthy development. There is an urgency to their sexual desires, and masturbation is an excellent outlet for that energy. It isn't enough to be coy and say that we understand or that "it's kind of rough being a teen." We need to help them deal with these feelings and urges <u>right now</u>.

Likewise, it would be helpful if we would be direct with kids about the value of non-genital caresses, kissing, massaging, cuddling. These are valuable life-skills which today's kids, in their rush to reach the goal of orgasm, are missing out on. These are the foundation of sensuality, a dying concept in a society racing to climax.

To think that masturbation and innocent touching will be enough is naive; adolescents' social development is accelerating, and their need and desire to feel emotionally connected with others is surging. That is why crushes and even young love, which can be amazingly intense, are such strong focal points in their lives. The adolescent years are a time to communicate your understanding of the wonder of being in love, validating their experience as a good one, and helping them distinguish between love and libido. Complement this attitude of respect for their emotional experiences with honest and direct exchanges about how their affection expressions are related to the present and their futures--individually and as a couple.

The concept of love has become so distorted that many of our children do not know that love is much more than arousal, and they need guidance if they are to learn the fine art of being lovers, which is primarily about how to be in relationship with another. Mature and successful adult models must be present for adolescents to discover that love's foundation is made up of the basic elements of friendship: trust, caring, honesty, sharing, etc. To be capable of creating and sustaining a deep friendship requires the building and maintenance of skills over an extended period of time. Learning the art of friendship becomes an education in the art of loving--dynamic tasks for the rest of their lives.

We are talking about helping our children move into the most exciting stage of the human experience: emotionally connecting with others at a rich and especially intimate level of sharing. This kind of sharing is what distinguishes great romances from good ones and what takes couples from terrific sex to celestial sex. This essential connection between friendship, commitment, and sexual intimacy has become terribly blurred. Your child needs for you to help him put it into a framework for his relationships now and later.

With minimal help, most teens and adults can respond to their urges and satisfy their basic genital longings. However, being a committed, creative, and caring lover is about intellectual, spiritual, and emotional exchanges, which are not so instinctively acquired. The challenging task is to help our children learn the art of imaginative and honest emotional sharing so that the love and romance in their lives will be a twenty-four-hour-a-day experience, not limited to a momentary thrill in the bedroom.

As you observe and share in your child's emerging puberty, talk about the incremental stages of intimacy. Help him to understand that each form of touching does not have to be part of a continuum, that each can communicate a unique feeling in the moment in which it is given. Stress the value of becoming adept with the basic behaviors of physical touching. For example, kissing is not merely a prelude to genital fondling. Kissing artists create "symphonies" with that one medium alone, and they can do so because they appreciate the act for itself and what they can communicate and experience with it, not for its investment value.

Assist your teen in appreciating that the more intimate the touching, the more aroused the partners become, and the more difficult it is for them to avoid risky behavior. Children need to understand this concept <u>before</u> they have steady dating partners. If you wait until they are "in love" to start talking about arousal and degrees of sexual touching, your child is very likely to view your remarks as being "against" their love or lacking in an awareness of what they view as their unique situation. What, to you, might be a neutral discussion about sexual arousal applying to everyone, may now be perceived as suspicion or interference.

As a society, we make the mistake of likening the teen love experience to mature, adult love. Teenagers have not yet completed their inner developmental work, and there is nothing which we can do to rush that work--even though this culture pushes them; it can only occur in nature's own time. So when we talk to our kids about the various levels of intimate sexual sharing, we need to take their lack of maturity into consideration. Because they are naturally so much more focused on the "I" rather than the "you" or the "we," they lack the ability to make decisions as rational as those whose development is further advanced. Our task is complicated because the cultural messages have led our teens to believe that they are, in fact, adults, that libido is love, and that sexual intercourse is an acceptable behavior for them if they are "careful."

This means that we walk a very delicate line as we try to address a subject which to them represents being adult. They do not respond well to messages which tell them that they ought not engage in "adult" behavior because they are too immature. I think that parents display much greater wisdom when they validate their children's strong feelings for their boy/girlfriends and talk about intimate touching in ways that acknowledge the pleasures, the risks, <u>and</u> the value and pleasure of non-genital touching. Our children are more inclined to consider our ideas when they perceive that we respect their emotional state within a relationship and that we are truly interested in them. The key, I believe, is in remaining empathic of your child's experiences and emotions and using the good feelings between you for occasions to broaden their perceptions. So long as they trust you as an ally, not an enemy, you are in a position to share your wisdom in a nonthreatening way.

Sex: The Great Communicator

I believe that it is especially important to talk about the correlation between the emotional investment one makes in a relationship and the level of intimate sexual sharing. This also is related to the difference between arousal and love. Sexual sharing needs to be placed within the context of commitment and caring, a novel concept for those whose exposure to sexual intimacy has been only physical passion.

Does the sexual intimacy one wants to express actually mirror the level of love, commitment, friendship, and emotional intimacy of the relationship? A very intimate sexual act (e.g., manual stimulation to orgasm) communicates a greater degree of investment and commitment to a relationship than one which is less private (e.g., deep kissing and non-genital caressing). Does our sexual sharing tell the truth about the emotional exchange between the participants, or is it simply physically gratifying for one or both partners?

Sexual intimacy is a powerful form of human communication which can be complicated by the compelling and pleasurable physical urges (arousal) which accompany the social and emotional feelings (love, neediness, etc.). To keep the sexual communication honest, a careful lover is very attentive to the emotional and social aspects of the relationship. Does the sexual expression match the level of interest in and commitment to the relationship? And are both partners at the same level?

Let your children know that sexual arousal is so incredible that the word "intoxicating" is sometimes used to describe it. Sexual sharing, as alcohol use, can easily get out of control. Alcohol use is known to give many individuals an inflated sense of their capabilities and power. Similarly, sexual intimacy's bonding properties cause people to feel closer to each other, more secure in their relationship than may actually be the case. Our children must become aware of sex's power to create feelings which do not necessarily have grounding in reality.

Help your children to understand that learning to be lovers is an art form and that one cannot become a great master by rushing. Again, we are talking about a process. To move quickly from hand holding to deep kissing is to rush things. So talk about some of your favorite, non-sexual dating moments and what made them so special. Speak to them about the events with your beloved that have communicated tremendous caring and which have been instrumental in your having those marvelously intense feelings of being treasured. And, above all else, keep those moments present and visible; they are proof that your verbal messages have validity.

I recall a scene in the movie, <u>Married to the Mob</u>, where the young F.B.I. agent spent the night with the attractive young widow with whom he was terribly enamored. They slept together; that's all. It was so tender and romantic, so obviously about a man who cared very much, who was sensitive to her feelings, and who had the capacity to find tremendous pleasure in being together, just holding each other. Take advantage of such scenes; they have tremendous power.

Speak about how easy it is for orgasm to become the focus of quiet moments together rather than time spent building fun memories and refining social skills. Surely you have examples around you of young couples who have let their friendships slide because they are so totally focused on being alone. It is akin to an addiction, putting everything else which was once important aside so that they can be alone to get physical. Does such isolation promote growth and happiness? How do our sexual choices relate to our goals for personal development as well as career aspirations? Talk together about what maturity in the individuals and what degree of friendship in the relationship should be present before the couple moves to a more serious level of sexual sharing.

This area is tricky. In our eagerness for intimate sexual sharing, all "lovers" tend to include themselves as eligible candidates; when a more objective observer would caution the couple to postpone advancing to deeper physical intimacy.

So help your children identify clear guidelines, relationship landmarks, if you will, when certain stages of sexual sharing are appropriate. Telling kids that sexual intimacy is "for adults," "mature people," those "in long-term relationships," or for "people who are really in love," does not help much. Those frequently-used expressions are so vague; what aroused fifteen-year-old doesn't believe that (s)he fits those descriptions?

Our ambiguous societal messages about relationships and sexual intimacy have left kids confused about an area of behavior where they desperately need clarity.

Discuss with your teens which characteristics they think the relationship and participants ought to possess before they reach the stages of:

- "French" kissing?
- touching a girl's breasts?
- cuddling stripped to the waist?
- manually caressing each other to orgasm?
- oral sex?
- engaging in acts which might make a baby?

Why?

- What do these acts communicate in addition to simple sexual pleasuring?
- How does a couple know if they and their relationship are ready for a deeper level of sexual behavior?
- What risks exist with each behavior, and are they, as a couple, at the stage where they can assume the ensuing responsibilities?
- What benefits will they enjoy (short-term and long-term) with each level of sexual pleasuring?
- Is it wise to make these decisions while aroused?

We must be very direct about the incredible power of arousal to alter our moods and judgment. It is vital to alert teens to be extremely cautious before taking the step to bring sexual pleasuring to orgasm into a relationship. I still believe that, for teens, stimulation to orgasm with their partners is not yet the best choice; it distracts the partners from the more complex and important undertaking of learning to become lovers in cooperative friendship. The relationship skills are so much more complicated and require years of social interaction to master. That refinement process is delayed, and for many is never completed, once the pleasure of orgasm distracts them by becoming part of the romance equation.

We all know many adults who have had multiple relationships that became sexual, but who have never enjoyed a mature, mutually-satisfying, lasting and committed romance. And we watch as each new relationship seems to take off with tremendous intensity but later falters because the partners, many years into adulthood, still lack the basic skills for creating real love. They still confuse the excitement of a new relationship, arousal, and love.

Our task is not easy. But it is necessary. We must stop pretending that kids are either holding hands and exchanging pecks or "going all the way," that there is nothing in between. We need to help them create some order about the messages all around them, the emotional feelings and physical sensations they are experiencing, how to build the skills to create and sustain lasting and committed love, and the enormous powers of sexually intimate behaviors.

I continue to believe that a trump card we overlook is our children's own goals of wanting a lifetime of committed love and happiness. If we can help them understand that they are making choices today and actively building the skills which affect their abilities to create the trust and love necessary for marital satisfaction, we will be adding meaning and purpose to their relationships. What is essential is that the <u>process</u> of becoming mature and adept is in itself a source of happiness. When parents help their adolescent children in this process, they are not viewed as kill-joys wanting to get in the way of happiness and fun; rather they are seen as understanding about feelings and urges, as people who demonstrate knowledge about, and even success with, satisfying relationships, and as friends who are willing to be honest about this aspect of maturation. Our kids will be more inclined to respect us as coaches who help them place the powerful sexual and social forces in a framework which can give pleasure today and tomorrow.

When the time is right, be willing to share with your children, the elements in your love relationship which you believe have been important in bringing you happiness:

- the activities which you can identify as important in your friendships with past and present partners;
- the forms of physical touching which you have found to bring you emotional contentment and comfort;
- occasions when one of your partners did not agree with or respect your preference regarding sexual intimacy; and
- feelings and the progression of your beliefs about sexual sharing.

For some kids, no amount of insight assists them in concentrating on the social skills; orgasm is their focus. If that is the case, how much better for them to have a basic understanding of the nuances of physical pleasuring and the non-intercourse options available so that they have a greater chance of staying out of the STD and pregnancy statistics. Just as important, those kids who stay just shy of sexual intercourse can walk away from broken romances with more of their emotional identities intact because the personal investment has not been nearly so great; this seems especially true for our daughters. Taking the step to sexual intercourse is a major one, a significant life event intimately connected with our individual identities.

Happiness and emotional connectedness are the lasting rewards of healthy relationships. Assisting kids to see that friendship is the core of love and that they can now participate in training to become more sensual men and women is a major task as we parent adolescents. Learning to be lovers is absolutely too important a part of our lives to be left hanging to figure it out in a society which bombards the unsuspecting with messages which are sexually saturated rather than emotionally and sensually balanced.

Chapter Twelve

PARENTS ARE PEOPLE TOO

While many chapters have been dedicated to helping you understand where your child is developmentally and then relating that stage to his/her sexual unfolding and awareness, your histories, attitudes, feelings, and examples have been equally important considerations. I want to summarize some points and highlight others to help you to become as comfortable as possible as you begin (or continue) this exciting journey.

So parents, keep in mind:

1.   That you are an expert, especially where your children are concerned. There is a subtle yet pervasive message to which so many middle and upper-income parents subscribe: professional experts with narrow specialties should be consulted whenever we experience doubts and difficulties in our parenting. We are still looking for someone with a magic wand to tell us how to raise the perfect child. There are some enormously talented professional people out there who can add insight, comfort, and advice, but <u>we</u> are the pilots, and <u>we</u> must assume a can-do attitude about our parenting abilities.

Learn to listen to your inner voice and trust yourself. There is no sex education genie who can or should serve as your substitute. Assistance, yes. But no one can take your place and, besides, your child is entitled to a parent who assumes responsibility and leads the way.

2. That sex really is more than a human plumbing lesson where we identify body parts, how they work, and explain how to avoid and fix plumbing-related problems. To do this we must accept that sexuality is so much more than what we do with our genitals, that it is about our basic identities and how we communicate that. So those who are capable, confident, and responsible demonstrate greater care, concern, and even pleasure when they do choose to express their sexual nature with their genitals.

It's time for us to recognize sexuality as an integral part of human life. We must allow our children to learn how to be happy with who they are and to become responsible as they go about living.

3. That no matter how "late" it seems, it is never too late to start talking about sexual behavior, feelings, thoughts, and attitudes with your children. Sure, it's easier when we start early, because then the conversations seem less personal and gradually become more sophisticated as the child gets older. But if nothing has been said before, now is the time to begin. Remember, it is never too late to say: "You know, when you were little, I was carrying around a lot of faulty ideas that told me we should never talk about sex. Maybe it's because my folks never talked about sex with me. Now I realize that such an important part of your life shouldn't have been neglected. I wish that someone had spoken with me about sex when I was a kid because I wondered about all kinds of things. Have you felt that way, too?" Then gradually use personal experiences or events in lives around you to start talking about sex.

If you and your child still read together, a carefully selected book (especially good fiction) can be a comfortable place to start. Judy Blume's books have provided some terrific opportunities for us to talk about menstrual periods, masturbation, sexual attraction, Peeping Toms, peer pressure, and the changing emotions of adolescence. Because her books introduce these topics within the context of someone's experiences, we are not just discussing biological facts or abstract ideas; we are talking about these matters as they relate to living. And that is what coming to terms with our sexuality involves--how it works in the real world.

4. That parents do not know everything about sex, and they haven't necessarily resolved all of their own confusion and questions. In order for parents to be useful resources for their kids, they need to accept themselves as healthy, sexual beings and then fill-in the information gaps.

Let's start with the information issue. Everyone will agree that parents must have basic sexual information clear in their own minds before they can be reliable sources for their children. There is a great deal of factual information that you understand correctly, and there has to be a lot that you don't. The nature of sexually transmitted diseases, for example, has changed dramatically in the last ten years. Trust yourself to share the knowledge that you have, and take advantage of the resources in your community when you are unsure. Libraries, bookstores, organizations, and agencies throughout this country are available resources which will help insure that the information you have is, in fact, correct.

- Most community colleges offer courses in human sexuality, covering everything from body parts, to body functions, to emotional responses. Many of these colleges permit people to register for just one course and to do so only for personal interest rather than for a grade. Many don't require a high school diploma.

- Public libraries are filled with books about the human body and, more specifically, human sexuality. Don't be embarrassed to ask for them or check them out. Seeking knowledge is never foolish, and library personnel are hired for the very task of assisting people with questions. You make their day more interesting when you approach them. If you want to do the footwork yourself, look under headings such as these: parenting, infants, toddlers, childhood development, adolescents, teenagers, sexuality, discipline, self-esteem, human body, birth control, homosexuality. The list is practically endless, and there are more materials than you could possibly ever use.

- County and city health departments have brochures and speakers. You've paid your taxes, so feel free to get the benefits.

- Look in your <u>Yellow Pages</u> under headings such as "A.I.D.S. information" and "birth control" and check out the "Blue Pages" of your phone directory's business section; the "Health Services" and "Family and Children Services" sections will have several listings to help you find the right organization or agency.

- Don't overlook organizations which advocate opposing views on important issues related to sexuality. Make serious inquiries with <u>both</u> sides. Every state has groups who serve as public advocates and educators regarding abortion, homosexuality, and sexually explicit material. If you don't know how to locate these groups, call the library or your local newspaper to get the names and phone numbers.
- Newspapers and magazines oftentimes include little "health notes." Clip those and talk about them with your child.
- Most churches/synagogues have lending libraries, bookstores, and staff or volunteers who can serve as resources and who might be better acquainted with you and your values.

Just remember, there are lots of sources for <u>facts</u>, but nobody else can put those facts in the context of values and give them a comprehensive meaning the way you can.

The second consideration that parents sometimes use as a roadblock to being their children's sexuality educators bears mentioning, too: unresolved issues. Some parents decide that their past struggles (e.g., having been sexually abused or having been raised in a family with alcoholism) excuse them from the role of sexuality educator, and that someone with "expertise" in this area or a less complicated personal history would do better.

Our sexuality will never be fully resolved because we are always in the process of development. No one has it all worked out. Your children cannot put their growth and development on hold while you work on your issues, so postponing your sharing is a disservice to them. Sexuality is about life, our attempts to clarify questions around us, and to live as fully as possible. How we model coping with uncertainties is an aspect of modeling our sexuality. Even if you "leave it to an expert," you are still teaching your kids about sexuality, and that message is that sex is so complicated that only experts, comedians, actors, and actresses can address it.

What we can do is to take steps to resolve our difficulties (e.g., self-help groups, counseling, reading) and to be honest with our children about our hopes and fears, our knowledge and ignorance, our doubts and confusion. A child's questions, which need answers, can be the stimuli for us to begin seeking answers for them and for ourselves. We can only do our best today.

5. That it helps to have a casual attitude and a sense of humor when discussing sex, just as you would when discussing the daily news. The early chapters in this book about romance, sexual intimacy, and our bodies can help you understand some of the impediments you might have to being comfortable about your own sexuality, and therefore your child's. The more relaxed you are with your beliefs and personal ways of expressing yourself, the less uptight you will be when talking about sexual matters.

Women, especially, have been socialized to respond disapprovingly whenever a joke is told or remark is made which has anything to do with sex. I suppose that responding so seriously was once considered proof of a woman's purity. Certainly, some jokes offend by degrading, but many reflect our vulnerability and contain elements of truth. It's okay to laugh when your child tells one of these jokes if you really find it funny. Humor is just one more way of expressing our delight, frustrations, curiosity, etc.

Keep in mind that each of us has appetites for food, drink, scents, touch, and sound. Our sexual instincts are not abnormal; the conditioning we have received to think that our sexual appetite is negative is what is abnormal. We are now in the process of breaking the chain that for decades had made sex an unmentionable subject and the source of so much guilt, shame, and embarrassment.

6. That kids prefer to talk to someone who respects their right to have opinions. Young people are exposed to many behaviors and values which you may find offensive. Examine and analyze the ideas your children toss at you without becoming upset or irritated with them. Sometimes, they are just needling you. At other times, they are trying on a new idea and seeking feedback from you. Treat these ideas like puzzles to solve rather than threats against which to gather arms, launch attacks, build fortresses, and shut out those with whom you disagree.

As you look at the issues, ask questions which prompt your child to take a closer look and to compare the outcomes of differing behaviors. If your child thinks you are frightened or threatened, your own position and esteem are weakened in his/her eyes.

7. That you may need to be the initiator for discussion, especially if sex is a subject that has been neglected. Invite conversation by asking questions about familiar situations, both in the real world and on television and in movies. During these conversations, give them your undivided attention.

I know one mother who is especially grateful for her phone-answering machine. When she and her kids are busy talking about something important, when they don't want the momentum broken, the answering machine guarantees that they can finish their conversation while still staying in touch with their friends. Her commitment to have their time uninterrupted tells her kids that their time together and the ideas they share are both important.

In some houses, conversations about sexuality will get started while family members are in the kitchen or TV room. Newspapers and magazines are frequently in view, and TV programming introduces numerous topics related to sex. Sometimes it is a joke which gets the conversation rolling. When an opportunity to talk about some aspect of sex presents itself, the parents try to pose questions that ask for more information than a <u>yes</u> or <u>no</u> answer. They listen carefully to the children's remarks and exchange ideas. Sex isn't treated as a subject any more important or delicate than any other. They just want to make sure that sex is not left out.

8. That your kids will feel safer expressing their true feelings if you model emotional honesty for them. Faking it is tough. It requires lots of extra energy, gives headaches, it makes our muscles tight, and is nearly impossible to hide. So if you feel uncomfortable when your kid asks: "Hey, Mom, what's a blow job?", it's perfectly all right to tell him that when you were a kid, parents and children rarely talked about stuff like that. Keep going. Tell him that this is a part of parenting that is new for you, and you are having to get used to it. Explain to him that you think sex is too important to bypass. You might even add that it's pretty exciting to get

to be honest and open with your kids. Then go ahead and answer the question. The more you do it, the easier it gets.

As kids get older, you may find that during discussions, they reveal acceptance of opinions and behaviors which are contrary to your beliefs. It is okay not only to tell them why you disagree, but you can also tell them how you react at a feeling level.

And be sure not to focus exclusively on all of the awful things which they might encounter due to unwise sexual choices. Talk about all of the neat things you observe in your children's lives today (be specific) and envision as you hear _them_ talk about what _they_ want in their futures.

This highlights a basic truth about teens: those who have nothing special in their lives must create something to fill the void. Too many attempt to fill the void with self-destructive activities. If your teen lacks an avenue for experiencing some form of success and personal meaning today, this is a red flag that (s)he needs help creating a more satisfying life--NOW.

Each time you offer your child an honest reflection which truly comes from the heart, you are more believable and are a more available human being, because you can talk about your feelings and theirs. You demonstrate that you have opinions, a value system, a deep interest in their happiness and well-being, a general willingness to listen and exchange ideas, that you are a valuable resource.

9. That you do not have to apologize for your values. They reflect who you are and what is important to you. If, for example, your value system supports sex within marriage as enriching and views sex outside of marriage as undesirable, then your moral code is not going to be in

agreement with most of the sexual situations that your children see on television and in the movies. Does that mean that you are wrong? Of course not. Share your beliefs. Explain why you believe as you do and how you see your values bringing more harmony and happiness to people's lives than values which you do not hold. I think that the key here is to demonstrate how your values enhance lives and actually free individuals to meet their potential. Too often, parents' values seem restrictive because of the manner in which they are presented. Semantics are mighty important. Just ask any political or legislative consultant.

10. That it is important to talk about the tough issues which are related to our sexuality. You may wish to ignore homosexuality and abortion and hope that they never come up in a conversation. They will, either with you or with someone else. There is much more in the news today than ever before about these and other difficult issues, and older kids, especially, want to talk about them. I strongly urge you to be an exciting example for your child and seek out resources from opposite viewpoints. Then critically evaluate the material you have reviewed together. See how differently you process the information and help each other.

An open mind, which is intrigued rather than intimidated, attracts ideas and people.

11. That if you ever suspect that a child is being or has been sexually abused, you take steps to protect that child immediately. Sometimes a parent covers for an abuser who is the only source of financial support for a family, believing that being on welfare or in a shelter is worse than the abuse the child is enduring. WRONG!

History is filled with examples of people who moved up from their destitute poverty to excel in business, government, entertainment, academics, etc. Sexual abuse destroys the very core of a child's emotional well-being, the foundation of his/her sense of worth. Unlike the victims of other physical abuses whose wounds are more readily visible, those who have been sexually abused are ravaged within. Even after the physical abuse has ended, the damage persists as if the mind had a terminally open wound.

If you knew that a neighbor had injured your child by knowingly hitting him/her with a car and then telling him/her to lie about what happened, would you again entrust your child to the neighbor's care, knowing that another "accident" might occur? Absolutely not. Would you overlook the evidence which led to your suspicions and just tell yourself that you were imagining things? No. So do not make excuses or give "second chances" to any individual whom you suspect of sexual behavior with a child.

This is a good time to mention that small children who are raised by teen mothers are more frequent victims of sexual abuse by boys and men who have not bonded with those children in a parent-child fashion. Such adults view these children not as individual human beings entitled to respect but as objects for sexual gratification. This situation can occur in any environment; it is unfortunate that such abuse is alarmingly frequent in teen-parent homes. So teen-parents need to be advised to be especially alert to such abuse.

Please be the parent and protector every child needs and deserves. If you are suspicious of abuse, make sure that it stops today.

12. That single parents raise sexually healthy children, too. A major difference in single parent families is that single parents model some additional roles. Consider:

- If they do not date, the child may want to know why.
  For parents who do date, what do they model about healthful courtship?
- Do they set the same standards of dating behavior that are set for teenagers? Why?
- Or do they distinguish between "adult" dating behavior and adolescent dating behavior? If so, why? Perhaps more importantly, how does the child process this explanation?
- Are there any differences in the dynamics of adolescent and adult relationships, and how do these relate to sexual intimacy?

Just as for married parents, what single parents do is just as important as what they say. In this respect, their children, too, need honest and consistent messages.

I must add here that there is a behavior I have repeatedly observed, usually in single-parent homes, and I have not seen it addressed in popular literature. This is the rotation of surrogate parent-figures (which I will describe shortly). Because it is not regularly discussed, I believe that in homes where it is occurring, the parent is unaware of its threat to his/her child's emotional well-being. And because the practice is so common and the results are so devastating, I am bothered that it has not yet become a major mental health issue. This is how it usually works and why I find it so disturbing:

The mother has a live-in boyfriend with whom her child bonds, just as the child would with an adopted father. Whether the child calls this figure "Daddy" or by his first name really doesn't matter. What is important is that the child has made a strong attachment to this "father figure." Because bonding is a natural process, a sign of health, the child is doing exactly what children are supposed to do.

After some time, when the relationship falls apart and the boyfriend leaves, the child feels abandoned--one of the most emotionally traumatic of childhood experiences. Children who have experienced what they perceive to be an abandonment have emotional scars that remain with them into adulthood. They have difficulty trusting people and allowing themselves to be vulnerable. Commitment may be nearly impossible for them. Their experience has taught them that it is foolish to entrust one's feelings to another human being. Consequently, they do not bond well in a marriage; yet they have no idea what is interfering with their happiness.

I have observed this rotation, mostly in children of single mothers, but it can happen to children raised by single fathers or in homes where one partner in a marriage walks out on the family. In the married case, I have also observed a parent who cannot make a commitment to either the family or the new romantic interest, so he goes back and forth. The results, no matter the particulars, are the same. The children feel abandoned and insecure.

Any major disturbance in a child's life, which undermines the developmental process and, thereby, his/her sense of self-worth and ability to interact well with others, interferes with the evolution of a healthy sexuality. Naturally, the greater the number of boy/girlfriends who live with a parent and then leave, the more deeply etched is the abandonment experience in the child's psyche.

This is a growing problem because of several factors: societal acceptance of unmarried cohabitation, more single parents, therefore more children affected, more teen mothers, and increasing emphasis on personal fulfillment, which sometimes comes at the expense of children's basic emotional needs.

Whether we are single-parent or two-parent families, children need secure environments where they are assured that they will be protected from harm and any threats of harm, where they will have their basic physical needs met, and where they will be loved and affirmed. Parents, whether single or married, who can give these basic essentials create environments where all family members can thrive and experience greater peace of mind as they go about the lifetime task of unfolding into healthy and mature human beings.

13. That sometimes parents face painful conflicts between their beliefs and traditions and their love for their children. It is not an easy time for families when children's lives clash with the moral codes of their parents. It is a struggle for each member, and the manner in which each copes depends upon the individual and the role (s)he plays in the situation. I'm talking about situations such as a daughter who has an abortion against her parents' wishes, teens who marry even with clear parental disapproval, parents whose children are gay or lesbian, unmarried children who cohabitate.

Sometimes parents say things like, "If any kid of mine ever does _____, I'll _____." We have no way of anticipating what lies ahead, and it is a waste of time to set out what we think we would do. Besides, until that moment, we really do not know how we are going to respond. Most people find that they experience many different emotions over a period of time when there has been a family upheaval.

If the unexpected happens, I hope that you are able to recognize that you are not the first family to experience these circumstances or this pain. Give yourselves time to process the information and make your decisions. And remember that you don't have to (nor is it always wise to) bail your child out or use your resources to support their choices. What is important is that you always remain an honest and empathic listener and friend. Good friends give honest and direct answers when asked for their opinions and advice. They also refrain from the urge to punish loved ones whose decisions are not in agreement with their own. That way the door is never closed, and the relationship is not so damaged that you can never be family again.

Support groups abound in the United States these days for parents of young and older children who have experienced just about every imaginable situation. And if there isn't one, you can always start one. Such groups can be your saving grace when you feel overwhelmed and don't know where to turn. You are never "the only one."

14. That there is no such thing as a "perfect parent." So be gentle with yourself when you make honest mistakes. Good parents actively try to do their best and accept that hindsight will always reveal some winners and some fumbles. If trouble in any given area continues and you can't seem to solve a problem yourself, don't hesitate to get professional

help or attend a support group. You are never the only person experiencing a given difficulty, so there is no need to feel embarrassed or ashamed of what people will think. These groups are usually anonymous (what is said there and who is seen there stays there), and the fellowship you will find in a group can be very reassuring and helpful.

For example, if you had little nurturing as a child, you may find that, contrary to your expectations, you are not even sure you like your child. That's not surprising, and it is not uncommon. But rather than do nothing about this situation and allow yet another generation in your family to suffer, seek help so that you can find peace and answers, and so that your child can get the emotional support during childhood that (s)he needs and deserves. Focus on what you do well, and expand on that rather than dwelling on your shortcomings.

15. That you cannot pour from an empty cup. In order to be emotionally available to your child you, too, will need emotional "fill-ups." Whether you get that from your partner, other friends, your faith community, you must get it. Becoming a parent and being committed to do that job well does not mean giving up oneself. That attitude fosters fatigue and resentment.

Make time for yourself and then use that time. This is not being selfish; it's being smart. Give yourself the gift of being around people who help you to feel good about who you are and what you do. This is why we have support groups such as Parents Without Partners. Such friends help you to feel renewed and assist you in visualizing yourself as a capable, contributing person.

If you can't afford a babysitter, join a babysitting cooperative. You need moments to refuel when you are not distracted from your own experience by someone else with needs or wants (e.g., your child). Besides, your regular departures and returns give your child opportunities to learn that (s)he can be happy and safe without you, that you always insure that she is well cared for while you are away, and that separations from you are followed by reunions.

Treat yourself as you would like a best friend to treat you. If you don't feel deserving, start with just one small gesture, and experience the pleasure of being loved and cared for. One woman I know started with a weekly manicure--something she had always wanted but had never been willing to give herself ("I shouldn't spend the money"). Not only will you feel more refreshed and renewed, you will have more reserves to be the loving parent you imagine yourself being, and you will give your child that priceless gift of modeling self-care and self-respect.

16. That today is the most important day of your life. Right now you can make choices and take active steps to give yourself the care you need and deserve, to be closer to your child, and to be the friend and parent you want to be. Each of us makes choices. We establish priorities, within the framework of finances, job status, support networks, etc. These largely determine the amount of time we can commit to our relationships. If you are waiting for your life and surroundings to be perfect before you can justify enjoying quality time with those who add meaning to your life, then you have established your priorities, and you may never enjoy the moments you seek.

We know a family whose children both started daycare as infants while the parents went to their jobs. This family did not have the finances to hire domestic help, so they kept their lives uncluttered with extra possessions and activities in order to insure that their time together really was "family time." Visiting their house, I never felt the tension of people trying to do or have it all. Their goals were few and clear, and they were successfully achieving them as they renewed their commitment to those goals on a daily basis.

Sometimes elderly and dying people teach the same lesson, but from a point of no return. Rarely do they talk about not selling a stock at the right time, not having a three handicap at golf, or not getting on the best committees at work. They lament missed opportunities for fun and caring with those who were special to them. Treasured memories and close relationships are not extravagances. They are the daily pleasures of those who understand our human need for love and belonging and who are willing to make the tiny choices each day which result in abundant affection and goodwill.

I encourage you to make regular reviews about what you are doing with life (or what you are letting life do with you) and to determine whether or not you and your loved ones are getting the "love time" which each of you needs and deserves. Choose carefully to create moments (however brief) which make memories, those simple, uncluttered twinklings when there is the time, space, and comfort to learn about and be about the art of living.

AFTERWORD

I have tremendous respect for the human will and our abilities to make choices and changes. I also observe that there are times when we become so enamored with the comforts and pleasures of our choices that we fail to realize the high price we are paying for these luxuries. For example, only quite recently the more industrialized societies have acknowledged the heavy environmental toll that our throwaway lifestyles demand. Similarly, I am not sure that we are aware of the spiritual and emotional prices we are paying for our concentration on, perhaps even obsession with, orgasm. While the magazines in the supermarkets guide us in our quest for more and improved sexual experiences, we find ourselves increasingly isolated from ourselves and our partners. We have a bigger and more explicit vocabulary for our sexual gymnastics, and we have climaxed in more positions and places than our grandparents dreamed possible, but at the same time we are expressing a discontent, an emotional emptiness which only love can fill.

I am hopeful that we will become more willing to take a careful look at our relationships, examine our pain and disappointments, and rechannel our sexual energy, expanding it to include more than the pleasures of sexual arousal. I hope that we will become willing to admit that we have neglected the art of loving, so taken are we by the awesome power of genital pleasuring. And just as our planet, the source of our material abundance, is now exhibiting signs of stress, so, too, are the partners in relationships who have confused simple passion for rich, nourishing, and lasting love.

I believe that nature provides so many parallels with our human experiences. Poets have mixed love and gardening for centuries. Drawing on their imagery, we might consider that beautiful flower gardens take time and attention. A gardener who does not understand soil and who fails to work in harmony with the local conditions will ultimately run into trouble. She might use the best weed killers, pesticides, and fertilizers and have a great growth the first few seasons but, in time, her insistence on an instant beauty will require more time, aggravation, and caustic elements to maintain any level of production. Satisfying, lasting relationships are no different. Instant intimacy, as instant flowers, feels just great at first and seems like the perfect formula; but as time passes, we find ourselves in the urgent position of decline because we neglected to take our time in understanding ourselves, our beloved, and learning to work harmoniously in our love environment with its unique conditions. We must first learn to grow and maintain the garden before we can expect to have the flowers and the inner peace to create magnificent floral designs for a lifetime.

Our children are the newest victims of this mentality which has little understanding of a natural order requiring couples to learn to be lovers first and sexual artists second. To offer them a vision of love and relationship which includes so much more than a quick high is to open the doors and show them paths to so much more celebration and so much less disappointment. If your own relationship experiences have been devoid of this greater intimacy, you can take steps now to gradually make them part of your reality. Rather than being your child's current proof of the rewards of patiently nurturing friendships which someday result in a lasting and committed love affair, you will be the adult model who teaches your child that it is never too late to take an honest look at our lives, reset our sights, make adjustments in the course, and pursue the happiness each of us is meant to have.

There are no guarantees in our lives, and there are none for our children's. What we can do is make choices which promote peace, growth, and satisfaction in our lives and those around us. Those of you who are willing to make room in your lives for a bigger and better image of human sexuality and who will then share that vision with your children, will be the answered prayers to the kids I meet who are begging for so much more than a "plumbing lesson." You have my admiration and gratitude.

Patty Stark
P.O. Box 670935
Dallas, Texas 75367-0935

March, 1991